THE BEHAVIOR CHANGE PROCESS

OSCAR G. MINK

THE BEHAVIOR CHANGE PROCESS

THE BEHAVIOR CHANGE PROCESS

Oscar G. Mink
West Virginia University

Harper & Row, Publishers
New York, Evanston, and London

 For information address Harper & Row, Publishers, Inc., 49 East 33rd Street, New York, N.Y. 10016.

Library of Congress Catalog Card Number: 76-103918

CONTENTS

PREFACE

The Behavior Change Process is self-instructional. It is a linear program combining constructed response and multiple-response format. It is designed to familiarize classroom instructors and counselors with a process for behavior change. In the applied psychological and pedagogical literature there are many possible approaches that could be taken to behavior change. In order to teach it well, it was necessary to take one specific process. The process which was chosen—reinforcement learning—has as much or more support in the empirical literature as any process for behavior change that one might share with teachers and counselors, and perhaps offers the most potential good for management of behavior change in the classroom, with the least potential harm to the student of any process approach that might have been selected (see Research Notes, pp. 169–183).

The Behavior Change Process was designed to help vocational instructors, teachers, and counselors to improve their effectiveness and interaction with individuals and groups in instructional as well as in a wide variety of group settings where they are in direct contact with students.

The Behavior Change Process includes adjunct prose, cases, research data, pre-, post-, and retention tests, and evaluative data. *The Behavior Change Process* is self-contained and can be used in teacher training programs, educational psychology classes, introductory psychology classes, and counselor education programs where instructors wish to expose their students to the rudiments of the process of behavior change. Since the reinforcement learning theory model was used as a basis from which to derive process concepts and sequencing, the program is oriented to that learning theory and is very specific yet as non-technical as possible.

In the writing, an attempt was made to keep the language simple and free of jargon, but at the same time such that it would back up the teaching of the concepts behind the more fundamental terms representing the key steps in the behavior change process.

O. G. M.

ACKNOWLEDGMENTS

In addition to Social and Rehabilitation Service units at the Federal, Regional, and State levels, many persons have contributed ideas and work on this program. Together they are too numerous to name, but there are several people who have made special contributions whom I wish to thank. Susan Zaslow Jackson labored long hours with me on the initial behavior chain as a result of early joint efforts in staff training at the Huntington Women's Job Corps Center. She wrote the first frames, many of which we later decided to discard but all of which helped make this work a reality. Julie Skinner Vargas, Associate Professor of Educational Psychology, West Virginia University, critiqued the second draft of the behavior chain and made several helpful suggestions. Performance Systems, Inc., developed the program to its field test form, including the cases, adjunct prose material, pre- and post-tests, and evaluation questionnaire. Irene Rubenstein, in consultation with Joe Tucker and Bernie Ulrich, was project manager. Herb Blumstein served as technical consultant, and Beverly Parks, assisted by David Blumstein, wrote most of the frames as presented in this manuscript. Richard Walls, Assistant Professor of Educational Psychology, West Virginia University, contributed the excellent research notes. Fran Stillman, Research Assistant, helped conduct the program evaluation effort. Finally, this investigation was supported in part by a research grant made available to the West Virginia Research and Training Center in Vocational Rehabilitation by the Social and Rehabilitation Service of the Department of Health, Education, and Welfare.

THE BEHAVIOR CHANGE PROCESS

PRE-TESTS

The following pre-tests are designed to test your knowledge of the behavioral chain explained in depth on the following pages. You are not expected to get all steps of the pre-tests in the proper sequence at this time, but try to do your best by ordering the sections in the way that would seem most logical to change behavior.

After you have completed the course, you will be interested to compare your scores on the pre-tests with your scores on the post-tests.

PRE-TEST A

Place the following in the most logical sequence to change behavior.

_______ Identify the behavior that you wish to eliminate and identify the new behavior that you wish to strengthen; hold a conference with the student.

_______ Identify the possible reinforcers for the undesirable behavior and determine who or what is providing the reinforcement for the undesirable behavior.

_______ Maintain the new behavior by using positive reinforcement, moving from a continuous reinforcement schedule to an occasional reinforcement schedule.

_______ Obtain suggestions from the student about ways to change his behavior; explain your own objections to his behavior; offer your own suggestions; consult with guidance services.

_______ Reshape the new behavior (if the old behavior recurs) and/or reexamine your past actions in the behavior change process.

_______ Decide upon a reinforcer that you think will strengthen the new behavior, and withhold the reinforcer for the undesirable behavior (extinction) or suppress the old behavior.

_______ Shape the new behavior.

ANSWER KEY

PRE-TEST A

1, 3, 6, 2, 7, 4, 5

INSTRUCTIONS: Circle the most correct alternative.

1. The first step in changing behavior of a student is to
   a. teach a new behavior.
   b. identify which behaviors you wish to eliminate and strengthen.
   c. extinguish or suppress undesirable behavior.
   d. discuss the problem behavior with the student.
2. Punishment may be successful in suppressing undesirable behavior, but it has possible side effects. Which of these alternatives is *not* considered a side effect of punishment?
   a. Punishment may be emotionally damaging to self-esteem.
   b. Punishment must be extremely drastic to significantly affect behavior.
   c. Punishment may be reinforcing the undesirable behavior.
   d. Punishment teaches the limits of acceptable behavior.
3. When holding a conference with a student about his undesirable behavior, what action can be taken then to encourage change?
   a. Punish him for his undesirable behavior.
   b. Obtain suggestions from him about ways to change his behavior.
   c. Praise him for the positive behavior he shows.
   d. Explain your own objections to his behavior.
4. Extinction of a student's behavior may best occur when
   a. the behavior is punished sharply and immediately.
   b. mild aversive stimuli is used so it is not damaging to the student.
   c. events that reinforce the undesirable behavior are removed.
   d. more positive behavior is reinforced.
5. When a student occasionally disrupts the classroom by making wisecracks, which alternative is the best to handle him?

a. Report him to the counselor.
b. Send him out of class.
c. Ignore his behavior.
d. Tell him to keep quiet.

6. Behavior is often changed through "shaping." Which of the following statements about shaping behavior is *not* true?

   a. Shaping is a gradual, training process.
   b. Behavior is made up of unconnected units.
   c. Desired behavior can be developed in a series of steps.
   d. Correct behavior is built up in small steps and strengthened until desirable behavior is reached.

7. If desirable new behavior is established and slips back into undesirable behavior, what action should first be taken?

   a. Ignore undesirable behavior.
   b. Reshape desirable new behavior.
   c. Punish undesirable behavior.
   d. Look for another desirable behavior.

8. Which is the most effective method of increasing the likelihood that a student will respond in a given way?

   a. Extinguish other responses.
   b. Have other students respond that way.
   c. Make the stimulus clear for the response.
   d. Reinforce similar responses.

9. The cause of recurrence of a particular misbehavior in school lies in

   a. effects of previous misbehavior.
   b. sibling rivalry.
   c. personality traits.
   d. the student's home background.

10. Continuous reinforcement schedules would be used in the behavior change process when

    a. new behavior is being shaped.
    b. new behavior is being maintained.
    c. undesirable behavior is being extinguished.
    d. behavior is being suppressed.

11. In reshaping (for the second time) new behavior, what action should *not* be taken?

- **a.** Reinforce desirable new behavior.
- **b.** Discuss the problem with the student.
- **c.** Punish undesirable behavior.
- **d.** Reconsider the reinforcements that were used.

12. Learning is a process that always brings about

- **a.** behavior that aids the person in his adjustment.
- **b.** improvements in the person's ways of perceiving or responding.
- **c.** increased variability in the person.
- **d.** changes in the way the person responds.

13. Occasional reinforcement schedules in changing behavior would be used when

- **a.** extinguishing an undesirable behavior.
- **b.** maintaining a new behavior.
- **c.** shaping a new behavior.
- **d.** suppressing behavior.

14. For reinforcement to be the most effective in learning, reinforcing experiences should occur

- **a.** after the lapse of a few days in order to permit the learned material to become established.
- **b.** immediately after the response.
- **c.** simultaneously with the learning.
- **d.** immediately before application is made.

15. Which of the statements about punishment is *not* true?

- **a.** Undesirable behavior is best weakened when the reinforcers which strengthen it are withheld.
- **b.** Punishment is the most effective way to weaken undesirable behavior.
- **c.** Punishment may temporarily stop undesirable behavior but may not change the behavior pattern.
- **d.** Behavior may be changed using methods other than punishment.

16. When a student is learning a new desirable behavior at school, he will learn it most quickly if he is reinforced
   a. occasionally (randomly).
   b. frequently.
   c. at regular intervals.
   d. continuously.
17. Learning takes place as a result of the individual's attempt to
   a. improve himself.
   b. conform to the expectations of his society.
   c. satisfy multiple motives and purposes.
   d. protect his self-esteem.
18. After a student has learned a desirable behavior, he should be reinforced
   a. occasionally.
   b. once out of every two times the behavior occurs.
   c. whenever the behavior occurs.
   d. not at all.
19. Which of the following steps of the behavioral change process is out of place?
   a. Identify behavior to be changed and new behavior.
   b. Hold conference with student.
   c. Identify possible reinforcers.
   d. Withhold reinforcer for undesirable behavior.
   e. none
21. You have determined some final behavior you want to strengthen. During the early stages of the process of shaping you must reinforce
   a. any response at all.
   b. a response that approaches the desirable behavior.
   c. only the final desirable behavior.
   d. positive and negative behavior both.
22. Repeated failure to reinforce a previously learned response is most likely to lead to
   a. the development of a strong habit.
   b. the elimination of an habitual response.
   c. striving for unrealistic goals.
   d. experimental neurosis.
   e. anxiety.

23. After desirable behavior has been learned, the undesirable behavior may occasionally reoccur. By not calling attention to the undesirable behavior, what method of controlling behavior is being used?

a. No behavior is being controlled at all.
b. punishment (negative reinforcement)
c. reinforcement of undesirable behavior
d. extinction

24. In the final stages of the shaping process (after new behavior exists), reinforcement should be given

a. occasionally.
b. whenever a response approaches desired behavior.
c. only when the new behavior occurs.
d. at regular intervals.

ANSWER KEY

PRE-TEST B

1.	b	7.	b	13.	b	19.	e
2.	d	8.	d	14.	b	20.	b
3.	b	9.	a	15.	b	21.	b
4.	c	10.	a	16.	d	22.	d
5.	c	11.	c	17.	c	23.	a
6.	b	12.	d	18.	a		

PRINCIPLES OF BEHAVIOR THEORY

The material in the following chapter is presented as an introduction to behavior theory. Its intention is to give you an understanding of reinforcement theory and to familiarize you with its terminology.

The section is designed to point out the relevance and application of behavioral psychology to the classroom. It is presented in essay form with self-check questions to help you discover what material you have learned and what material requires further study. You should understand these concepts **before** going through the self-instruction program.

What is behavior?

The field of psychology emerged as a discipline which concerned itself with the inner workings of the mind. At first, psychology was not considered a science; it was closer to the field of philosophy. Today, there are many psychologists who still focus mainly on the inner workings of the mind. There is one school of psychology, however, that has moved psychology into the laboratory; and, in so doing, this school has changed the focus of psychology from the study of the mind to the study of *behavior*.

The emphasis of psychologists who study behavior is not on the nonobservable inner workings of the mind, but rather on activity that can be observed in the form of actions and responses. Behavioral psychologists are working to discover what makes animals and people act the way they do. They hope eventually to identify more precisely the conditions under which people will respond in the most effective way as individuals and as members of society.

The term *behavior* is precisely defined as any action that can be observed or measured in some way by others. This definition raises the question: Is "the act of thinking" behavior? The behavioral psychologist would say No, since thinking is something that only the thinker himself can experience. No one else can observe or measure this process directly.* The act of thinking is behavior only when the thinker says something or writes something about his thoughts, or acts them out in pantomime, song, dance, or other observable actions. The term "feeling" is similar to the word "thinking." Take a description such as, "Bob feels sad" (he may have been crying; he may be pouting), or "Bob says he is sad"—these are the observable behaviors.

A non-behaviorist might say: "Sandy fears the dark." A behaviorist would say: "She avoids going into a darkened room;

*Behaviors that cannot be observed or measured are called *covert behaviors*. Covert behavior applies to inner processes that cannot be described scientifically. Behavior that can be observed and measured is called *overt*.

she trembles when she is in a darkened room; a dark room brings on increased perspiration; Sandy cries when she is left in the dark." For the behaviorist, fear is a term which has no objective meaning. Only the actual behavior can serve as evidence of "Sandy's emotional state."

A non-behaviorist might say, "Ralph is a self-conscious person." A behaviorist would describe Ralph's behavior in terms of the following overt responses: "Ralph blushes when people talk to him; Ralph twitches in his seat when he is in a group; Ralph is constantly seen to readjust his clothing when he is around other people."

There is not one set of responses to describe self-conscious behavior or fear or anger. The behavioral psychologist, however, identifies the actions which he observes. He does not wish to generalize about behavior with labels such as "fear," for descriptions such as this do not describe what the person is actually doing.

Of course, in everyday conversation you use adjectives such as "angry" and "fearful," or verbs like "think" and "feel." In this discussion, we are stressing the use of behavioral language not to make you feel self-conscious about carrying on an ordinary conversation concerning your students with your friends and colleagues, but rather to emphasize the fact that when you want to identify a student's behavior exactly, the behavior that you can describe with any degree of certainty is that behavior that you can observe. When you really get down to the problem of changing behavior, it is important that you have, in fact, really described *behavior*.

1. In each group below, check the items that a behavioral psychologist would call behavior:

☐ **a.** laughing
☐ feeling happy
☐ smiling

☐ **b.** feeling dejected
☐ crying
☐ saying, "I am dejected."

☐ c. speaking of justice
☐ thinking of justice
☐ believing in justice
☐ d. giving the answer to a linear equation
☐ understanding a linear equation
☐ writing a linear equation
☐ e. marking the musical passages one says he likes
☐ enjoying passages of music
☐ selecting a favorite record and listening to it
☐ f. grasping the theory of relativity
☐ explaining the theory of relativity
☐ making predictions based on the theory of relativity
☐ g. knowing about the weather
☐ making predictions about the weather
☐ understanding weather maps

2. Check the following activities which would be considered observable:

☐ a. knowing someone's name
☐ b. seeing a movie
☐ c. listing the groceries
☐ d. planning a trip by discussing it with someone
☐ e. feeling depressed
☐ f. knowing the answer
☐ g. thinking about the answer
☐ h. writing a conclusion
☐ i. recognizing a person and calling him by name
☐ j. identifying a problem by talking about it with someone
☐ k. selecting a book from a shelf
☐ l. enjoying a record

The following is an interesting example of the way behavioral psychologists handled a problem involving human behavior.

The patients in a psychiatric hospital were very slow in coming to meals. It often took the staff as long as an hour after the dinner bell had rung to get many of them into the dining room. The problem was turned over to a group of behavioral psychologists to solve. They investigated the circumstances which brought about the undesirable behavior and discovered that the patients were ignored most of the time and had nothing to do to keep busy. They were generally bored. Meal times gave them the only opportunity to get attention. Since the attendants had to escort them, they could give the attendants a hard time by using delaying and dawdling tactics. This was a type of negative attention-getting behavior. The psychologists decided to reduce the oportunity for this attention-getting behavior.

They set up a new dining room procedure. On the first day, 20 minutes after the dinner bell had rung, the dining room doors were locked and no one else could enter the room. Those patients who had not arrived by this time did not eat. Each day the doors were locked after a shorter period of time. Those patients who got to the dining room on time ate; the others had to wait for the next meal. The result was that everyone finally got to the dining room five minutes after the bell rang, and they walked in by themselves without the need for the attendants to escort them into the room.*

In the above case, the psychologists were interested in changing behavior. They began by analyzing the patients' undesirable behavior, that is, coming late to the dining room, to determine what advantages the patients were getting out of behaving in this way, and found out that the patients could get special attention from the attendants in this way. Then they determined the desired behavior and how to create conditions that would bring about this desired new behavior.

The method of dealing with the patients in the mental hospital, as described above, seems rather simple and mechanical —ringing bells, giving people a time limit, and then locking

*This example was reported in the *New York Times Magazine*, March 17, 1968, pp. 27–29.

doors. It sounds like a very mechanical way in which to handle people. But it can be argued that the patients' new behavior was more desirable not only from the viewpoint of the hospital attendants but also the patients themselves. Their facial expressions and manner of walking indicated a new attitude of dignity and confidence.

The patients are left, in this account, with no further attempts to fully work out their problems, the immediate problem having been resolved. We can go on from there. What about the lack of attention to them during the day? What about more constructive ways of getting attention? It would now be necessary for the hospital staff to provide the necessary opportunities for the patients to become involved in activities, and to develop meaningful relationships with the attendants.

SUMMARY

There are many schools of thought in psychology today besides the school of behavioral psychology; however, our emphasis here is on behavioral psychology, because this point of view provides a direct way of dealing with problems you may encounter in the classroom. As a teacher, you are in the role of behavioral psychologist when you are identifying, describing, evaluating, and changing student behavior. You are in the position to mold desirable behavior and change behavior which you think is undesirable. You must, therefore, be able to define clearly the behavior that already exists and to decide what new, desirable behavior you want to develop in your students.

A student is behaving by **raising** his hand, by **answering** a question (whether his answer is correct or incorrect), by **sitting,** by **doodling** on a piece of paper, by **asking** a question (whether it is a silly or an intelligent question), by **writing** answers to questions, by **building** a piece of equipment, by **wandering** around the room. The emphasized words represent the observable actions or behaviors. Some are desirable and others are undesirable, but all of them can be observed; that is, they can be identified and described. Some behavior may be desirable under certain conditions and some other behavior may be undesirable under some conditions, but all observable actions, whether they are right or wrong, good or bad, make up behavior.

How can we talk about behavior?
When a student is described as a "behavior problem," it usually means that he is behaving in an undesirable way. When someone says that a child "misbehaves," he does not mean that the child is not behaving, he means that the child **is** behaving, but behaving in a way that is contrary to what adults would like his behavior to be. The term "misbehavior" is vague because it does not specify the behavior that is undesirable. If we want to change problem behavior into desirable behavior, the undesirable behavior must be described clearly, as well as the behavior with which we would like to replace it. As an instructor, you are continually called upon to describe the behavior of your students by evaluating their performance on class assignments or the way they get along with classmates or with you.

It is most important that your descriptions give a clear picture of the student's behavior. Let's analyze the following evaluation:

> Bob is only a fair student. He wastes time and doesn't complete his work.

This description raises several questions. It does tell us what Bob does not do, but it does not tell us what Bob actually *is* doing. What is Bob doing when he is wasting time? Is he wandering around the room or is he simply staring out the window or is he talking to a classmate? Since you want Bob to use his time more wisely, you should begin by identifying Bob's specific undesirable behavior and then help him change this "wasting time" behavior into more purposeful activities. The above description also tells us that Bob is only a "fair" student. The term "fair" doesn't describe Bob's behavior. Both you and he should identify just what he is doing that is incorrect or inadequate and then define the exact criterion for what is correct or acceptable behavior so that both you and he can measure his performance against this criterion.

Here is a case in point:

> A mother yells at her son as he tramps into the house with wet boots, "Bobby, don't leave your wet boots in the

middle of the kitchen floor." Now Bobby has learned where not to leave his boots, but this doesn't direct him to what he should do instead. It would be much more efficient and effective if his Mother had said, "Bobby, leave your boots here" (pointing or telling him precisely where wet boots are to be left).

If you describe a student by saying he has "bad manners," you have not told what the student actually does. The term "bad manners" is a general form of undesirable behavior, but does not specifically identify the particular behavior. Does this student interrupt you? Does he use an offensive tone of voice? Does he annoy other students? These are observable evidences of "bad manners." If you want to help a student change his behavior, it will be most helpful if you first identify exactly what the student is doing, and then identify as precisely as you can what you would rather have him do instead. Your emphasis, both when you identify the student's undesirable behavior and when you identify the behavior with which you would like it replaced, should be on observable actions which can be described concretely.

3. Check the following statements that describe a student's behavior as the behavioral psychologist would describe it:

☐ **a.** Frances needs attention.

☐ **b.** Janet attends to her work for only very short periods of time; most of the time she stares out the window.

☐ **c.** Sue helps other students when they have questions.

☐ **d.** Sam is easily distracted. He often stares out the window when he sees activity or hears noises.

☐ **e.** Joseph is not able to compute long division problems correctly.

☐ **f.** John has emotional problems.

☐ **g.** Ralph frequently argues with his classmates.

☐ **h.** Jane feels picked on.

☐ **i.** Robert doesn't understand directions.

4. Restate these descriptions as a behaviorist would describe them:

a. Joe is a discipline problem.

b. Fred enjoys baseball.

c. Janet doesn't understand directions after they have been given.

d. Frank does not do well in typing class.

e. Paul has a poor attitude.

SETTING BEHAVIORAL OBJECTIVES

What do we want the student to do?
Learning is the process of acquiring new behaviors. The instructor's role in this process is to provide the materials, the information, the activities, and any other conditions that enable the learner to acquire new behaviors most effectively. Therefore, every course should describe its goals or objectives in terms of the new behavior(s) which each student should acquire by the end of the course.

Let's look at the following course objective:

> This course in Electrical Repair will provide the student with an **understanding** of electricity and the **knowledge** of repairing appliances such as washing machines, refrigerators, dryers, and electric ranges.

Notice that the words "understanding" and "knowledge" were emphasized. These terms do not describe activities that are observable or measurable. A teacher can only evaluate whether or not a student understands something by watching what the student does, listening to what he says, or reading what he writes. The only evidence the instructor has that a student understands electricity or knows appliance repairing would be whether or not the student could do some or all of the following: wire a piece of equipment correctly, draw and explain a wiring diagram, or fix a washing machine so that it works properly. The behaviors that are observable and capable of being evaluated in the above example of the electrical repair course were not "understanding" and "knowing," but rather **wiring** and **fixing.** Since students will be evaluated on their skill in performing these activities, it would be better to express the objectives in terms of the actual behaviors. The objectives for the Electrical Repair course might have been stated in the following way:

> At the end of this course in Electrical Repair the student should be able to perform the following: **read** a wiring diagram; **wire** the following appliances correctly: washing machines, dryers, electric ranges, refrigerators; **identify** all parts of each appliance; **locate** the source of a problem in a defective appliance; and **fix** faulty appliances so that they operate effectively.

This is a workable list of behaviors by which an instructor can measure his students' "understanding" and "knowledge" of the required concepts and skills.

In addition to the words "understanding" and "knowing," the word "appreciate" is often used in statements of course objectives. This word, too, tells us little about the new behavior. We cannot observe the student's appreciation of good music. But we can observe him saying he likes a certain type of music—listening to a recording of Beethoven's 5th Symphony, tuning in Herb Alpert on the radio, buying a Beatles record, or going to hear the New York Philharmonic. In other words, talking, listening, tuning, buying, and going are the observable behaviors which provide the basic evidence for saying that a person appreciates music. If you were teaching a music course, instead of stating that you plan to teach your students to appreciate music it would be more precise to say that you plan to teach your students: **to listen to** a variety of musical styles, such as chamber music, oratorio, and opera; **to recognize** different musical forms, such as the sonata, the fugue, and the symphony; and **to identify** different musical instruments by their sounds. As the teacher of this course, you might hope that a student who acquired these behaviors would demonstrate his appreciation by going to concerts, buying records, listening to music, and so on.

By defining the desired new behaviors, you have described what the learner must do to reach his goal. It can be further specified by telling him how well you want him to be able to perform the task. Consider the following statement of an objective for a course in typing:

a. to be able to type
b. to be able to type 80 words per minute

If you are only concerned with teaching the mechanics of typing (pressing the proper keys), objective "a" would be sufficient; but if you desire that a certain degree of skill be reached, that should be clearly stated in objective terms, that is, in words per minute.

In a course on Auto Body Repair, for example, a student is to demonstrate that he can weld metal. The standards for an acceptable welding job should be clearly defined so that the student can measure his performance as he is acquiring this skill.

5. Which of the following objectives are stated in behavioral terms?

a. For an accounting course:
- ☐ to understand accounting principles
- ☐ to write financial statements; to make accurate computations whenever necessary

b. For a course in radio repair:
- ☐ to label all the parts of a radio; to describe the function of each part; to identify a problem and fix it
- ☐ to know how a radio works and repair any defective parts

c. For a book on how to play chess:
- ☐ to know the rules of chess
- ☐ to play the game of chess

d. For a reading course:
- ☐ to know the main idea of the story
- ☐ to state the main idea of the story

Up to this point, we have been concerned with the problem of defining what new behavior is expected of the student and defining the minimum standard for his performance. The objective should also include important information such as the conditions under which the student's performance will be tested or evaluated. For example, in our music course, one of the behavioral objectives was that the student be able to recognize a sonata. There are many possible ways of testing the ability to recognize sonata form. The teacher might play a sonata and ask the student to name the form. He might ask the student to pick out a sonata from a short selection containing several musical forms, or he might play a sonata and ask the student to choose the correct form among a list of many musical forms. Each of these conditions presents an entirely different problem for the student.

The objective should include the conditions under which the student's performance will be tested. It could be expressed this way: Given a list of musical forms, the student will be expected to select the correct form from the list after listening to an unidentified short selection of music.

In a sewing course, if you want to teach a student to make a finished garment from an uncut piece of cloth, the course objective might be stated this way: Given a printed pattern, the student must be able to adjust the pattern to fit herself, follow the pattern directions, lay out the pattern, and cut it and assemble it correctly. This objective tells us not only what **is** required, but also that the student will start with a ready-made pattern and will **not** have to design her own.

If you teach a course in remedial arithmetic and a student is having particular difficulty memorizing his multiplication table, you might be satisfied if he did not commit these facts to memory. You might decide that this student can refer to his multiplication tables for the facts needed to do multiplication problems. For this student the objectives would be stated: to be able to compute accurately multiplication problems of the form (23 × 45 =) with the use of a multiplication table.

SUMMARY

A. Behavioral objectives should state what the student is required to do at the end of the course. The performance should be stated in terms of observable behavior.

B. The objective should also state the minimum standard for success, that is, how well the task(s) should be performed.

C. The objectives should also state the conditions under which the student will be tested or evaluated.

6. Which of the following contain the three criteria for stating an objective behaviorally?

   a. History course:

   - ☐ The student should know the causes of the Civil War.
   - ☐ When tested on a written examination, the student should be able to list at least nine different causes of the Civil War.
   - ☐ When required on a written examination, the student should be able to select the four main causes of the Civil War from a list.

   b. Horticulture course:

   - ☐ The student should demonstrate that he is able to select and use the appropriate tools to perform the following: pruning, weeding, trimming, and bed preparation; the student should be able to identify different soil types and select the appropriate fertilizer for each when presented with samples.
   - ☐ The student should know the different fertilizers and know when to use the correct fertilizer for the various soil problems.

7. Construct a well-stated behavioral objective to teach someone the rules of the road and to teach a student to drive a standard gear-shift automobile. Be certain to state what the student should be able to do, the minimum standard for success, and the conditions under which the student's performance will be evaluated at the end of the course.

ANSWER KEY

DEFINING BEHAVIOR

1. a. laughing
   smiling
   b. crying
   saying "I am dejected."
   c. speaking of justice
   d. giving the answer to a linear equation
   writing a linear equation
   e. marking the musical passages one says he likes
   selecting a favorite record and listening to it
   f. explaining the theory of relativity
   making predictions based on the theory of relativity
   g. making predictions about the weather

2. b. seeing a movie
   c. listing the groceries
   d. planning a trip by discussing it with someone
   h. writing a conclusion
   i. recognizing a person and calling him by name
   j. identifying a problem by talking about it with someone
   k. selecting a book from a shelf

DESCRIBING BEHAVIOR

3. b. Janet attends to her work for only very short periods of time; most of the time she stares out the window.
   c. Sue helps other students when they have questions.
   d. Sam is easily distracted. He often stares out the window when he sees activity or hears noises.
   e. Joseph is not able to compute long division problems correctly.
   g. Ralph frequently argues with his classmates.

4. The following are possible answers. Your answers may be quite different from the ones given below, which appear

here as guidelines you can use to evaluate your own behavioral descriptions.

a. Joe comes late to class.
Joe talks out of turn.
Joe is aggressive and unfriendly to his classmates.

b. Fred plays baseball very often.
Fred watches baseball on television at every opportunity.
Fred attends the baseball games in town whenever he can.

c. Janet does not begin to work when directions have been given.
Janet says she does not understand directions.
Janet's work has many errors.

d. Frank types ten words per minute with two errors.

e. Paul does not do his assignments.
Paul sits in class and has a blank expression on his face.
Paul uses an impolite tone of voice when he speaks to his teachers.
Paul is frequently late for class.

SETTING BEHAVIORAL OBJECTIVES

5. a. to write financial statements; to make accurate computations
b. to label all the parts of radio; to describe the function of each part; to identify a problem and fix it
c. to play the game of chess
d. to state the main idea of the story

6. a. History course:

When tested on a written examination, the student should be able to list at least nine different causes of the civil war.

When required on a written examination, the student should be able to select the four main causes of the civil war from a list.

b. Horticulture course:

The student should demonstrate that he is able to select and use the appropriate tools for pruning, weeding, trimming, and bed preparation.

The student should be able to identify different soil types and select the appropriate fertilizer for each when presented with samples.

7. The following is a possible answer. Use it as a guideline for evaluating your own.

The student should be able to answer 18 out of 20 questions about the rules of the road correctly.

The student should be able to identify all road signs correctly.

After stopping and starting 5 times, the student is to operate the automobile for 15 minutes without stalling more than once.

CHANGING BEHAVIOR

How do we **weaken** *and* **eliminate** *undesirable behavior?*
John is a 22-year-old, physically handicapped man who is studying to be an accountant at the vocational rehabilitation center. His instructor finds John very alert and intelligent when they talk together privately, but he does not participate in class discussions. The instructor has observed that John is unwilling to volunteer answers in class or to talk with other students. The teacher wants to build up John's self-confidence so that he is able to answer questions and to participate in other classroom activities. This teacher is trying to change John's classroom behavior. Before reading on and discovering how this teacher changed John's behavior, take a minute to decide what you might do in this situation.

John's teacher felt that she had to help John gain self-confidence so that he would be able to answer correctly and make himself understood in class. She decided on the following method. She called on John as frequently as she did everyone else so that John would not feel as though he were being singled out. When John had trouble answering, she would praise him for every correct or partially correct response. She might say, "Very good, John," or "That's excellent, John," or "Very well done, John." Incorrect answers were treated nonchalantly. John was encouraged to reevaluate any wrong answers by statements such as, "That's not bad, but perhaps we can get a better answer, John," or "Let's try to look this question over again," or "I believe we can do better, John." In all cases, the teacher rewarded John's attempts by using apropriate words or phrases of praise to boost his confidence. This method of publicly rewarding his correct answers *reinforced* John's self-confidence and he started participating more and more in class.

This method of changing behavior by rewarding the behavior that you wish the student to exhibit is called *positive reinforcement. Reinforcement* is any stimulus (praise, food, water) that will increase or maintain the strength of a response associated with it. Therefore, if we wish to reinforce a behavior, we must discover which stimulus (praise, food, etc.) will maintain or increase the strength of the response that we are seeking. Positive reinforcement is the use of a stimulus that, when added after a behavior, strengthens the probability of that behavior's occurring again.

Positive reinforcement can be used in the classroom by following these three steps:

1. Determine the behavior you want the student to exhibit.
2. Select the reinforcer that will increase the probability of this behavior's occurrence and wait for the student to exhibit this behavior, that is, answering in class, raising his hand, or handing in neat work.
3. Apply the reinforcer when the desired behavior is exhibited; that is, praise him for a work well done, with a commendation such as "You answered very well," or "Thank you for raising your hand," or "This work is excellent."

Now see if you understand this idea of positively reinforcing a behavior. If you have difficulty in answering any of the questions below, go back and reread the section which explains the answer.

1. What behavior was John's teacher trying to get John to perform?

2. How did John's teacher accomplish this?

3. What is this method of changing behavior called?

4. What was the positive reinforcer in John's case?

5. What does the positive reinforcer do?

6. Name some other positive reinforcers.

7. Describe the steps in applying positive reinforcement.

Positive reinforcement is not the only method by which a teacher may change a student's behavior. At the turn of this century behavior change was accomplished, sometimes effectively, by a hickory switch. This form of behavioral control is known as punishment, a form of *negative reinforcement.* Negative reinforcement is the application of an aversive stimulus (pain, embarrassment, fear) in order to suppress an undesirable behavior.

Another way of eliminating an undesirable behavior is the removal of the positively reinforcing stimulus that is maintaining that undesirable behavior. The removal of positive reinforcement for a specific response is called *extinction*. It is the most important method for weakening or eliminating a response. Extinguishing a behavior is the opposite of positively reinforcing a behavior. Instead of trying to strengthen the behavior, we are trying to erase it. Let's look at a classroom situation where we want to "extinguish" an undesirable behavior:

> Lucille is an emotionally handicapped girl of 17 who is studying accounting at the vocational rehabilitation center. Lucille constantly disrupts the class by abruptly leaving her seat and pacing back and forth between other students' desks.

Stop here and consider how you would go about eliminating this undesirable behavior of Lucille's.

Now let's examine one way to change Lucille's undesirable behavior. First, we will use the method of applying an aversive stimulus. In this case, we could have used aversive stimuli such as

a. threats to report Lucille to her counselor.
b. threats to eject Lucille from the class.
c. threats to lower Lucille's grades.
d. threats to withhold graduation approval.
e. simple shouting.
f. embarrassing her before the class by belittling her.
g. physical action (hitting).

Any of these stimuli is punishing to the student and may be successful in suppressing an undesirable behavior. However, it should be noted that this form of behavioral control is not advisable to use because of its possible side effects. The use of such stimuli may be emotionally disturbing to the student. They may be damaging to a student's self-confidence and self-esteem, and this would be a high price to pay for eliminating the behavior. Moreover, it has been shown through numerous independent experiments that the application of aversive stimuli must be extremely drastic to affect significantly the student's behavior. A third drawback of this method is that we may be accidentally reinforcing Lucille's need for attention, so that instead of extinguishing the behavior, we are actually strengthening it.

To summarize this aspect of negative reinforcement, we can state that the application of aversive stimuli in the form of physical or mental hurt is effective usually only if the aversive stimuli are exceptionally drastic. For example, we may (hypothetically, of course) threaten Lucille with ejection from school and placement in a reformatory instead. This may put an end to her antics; but it may also frighten her to the degree that she becomes emotionally upset to the degree that she is unable to function properly at all. The other alternative is to use a mildly aversive stimuli, so as not to upset Lucille emotionally; but this means that there is less chance of behavioral change occurring.

Using the method of extinction in Lucille's case, it is necessary to remove the events that are currently reinforcing her undesirable behavior. Let us assume that Lucille's disruptive activity is reinforced and strengthened when she is given attention during one of these disruptions. If this is the case, then attention is the positive reinforcer that is strengthening her disruptive behavior, and it must be removed.

As an example, we may say that Lucille's behavior may be extinguished by *not* reinforcing her disruptive behavior. This may be accomplished by

a. ignoring her antics and continuing the lesson.
b. instructing the class to pay no attention to her.

If attention is truly the reinforcer for Lucille's disruptive behavior, her behavior will be reinforced less and less, eventually leading to the extinction of her disruptive behavior.

One of the problems that you may come upon is the reoccurence of the undesirable behavior after a long period during which you believed that the behavior was permanently changed. In this case it is necessary to reestablish your reinforcement methods and review your basic perceptions of the student's problems. Your initial identification of the reinforcers that were maintaining the undesirable behavior may have been faulty, or you may not have correctly identified the reinforcers that would successfully strengthen the desirable behavior.

SUMMARY

You have studied three different ways to change behavior:

1. positive reinforcement—applying a rewarding stimulus when a desired behavior is performed, so that this behavior is strengthened.

2. negative reinforcement—punishing by applying aversive (painful, uncomfortable, etc.) stimuli.
3. the process of extinction—withdrawing the positive reinforcement of the undesirable behavior.

But usually behavior change is effected when a combination of different methods is used. In Lucille's case, two processes might be combined:

1. extinction—ignoring Lucille's antics.
2. positive reinforcements—rewarding her when she is working quietly and efficiently.

This would enable Lucille's teacher simultaneously to eliminate the disruptive behavior and strengthen the desirable behavior.

To be able to use combinations of methods of behavioral change takes a good deal of perception on your part. It is by no means a mechanically perfect method and is subject to some disappointments and failures.

Answer the questions below to see how well you understand the process of weakening and eliminating undesirable behavior.

8. Name two ways of eliminating undesirable behavior.

9. What was Lucille's major problem that needed extinguishing?

10. What reason was given for Lucille's disruptive classroom behavior?

11. What are the drawbacks of applying aversive stimuli to extinguish behavior?

12. Name four kinds of aversive stimuli.

13. How was Lucille's problem finally worked out?

ANSWER KEY

CHANGING BEHAVIOR

1. answering in class
2. praising John publicly whenever he attempted to answer in class
3. positive reinforcement
4. the words of praise
5. It strengthens the occurrence of the behavior associated with it.
6. food, water, and social acceptance, etc.
7. **a.** Decide on the behavior you want to strengthen.
   b. Select a reinforcer to strengthen the behavior and wait for the behavior to occur.
   c. Apply the reinforcer when the desired behavior is exhibited.
8. **a.** applying aversive stimuli—punishment
   b. removing positively reinforcing stimuli—extinction
9. disruptive behavior
10. need for attention

11. **a.** need for very drastic measures
    b. It may be emotionally damaging.
    c. It may be actually reinforcing Lucille's wish for attention.
12. **a.** physical pain
    b. embarrassment
    c. threats
    d. scolding
13. by ignoring her disruptive behavior (extinction) and by positively reinforcing the desired behavior

SHAPING BEHAVIOR

How do we bring about **new** *behavior?*
Behavior is made up of a continuous series of responses. Walking, talking, writing, computing a math problem, building a radio—any behavior you can name is really a series of skills which are built slowly, one upon the other. The final behavior does not come about all at once; rather, it develops in stages through a process known as **shaping.** New responses (behaviors) can be added to a person's repertoire and old responses can be changed or eliminated through the shaping process.

The process of shaping is very much like the work of the sculptor, who literally shapes an unformed material into some desired form. The material which the sculptor uses goes through a variety of preliminary forms leading to the finished piece of art. Behavior can also be shaped into some desired form. It, too, must undergo many preliminary stages before it reaches its final form. A common example of the shaping process is a child's learning to talk. At first the child makes random sounds which receive various kinds of reinforcements from the adults around him, such as broad smiles and claps of delight. These social reinforcers strengthen the baby's sound-making behavior. At one time or another the baby will make a noise which the adults around him will interpret as a real word. The sound will probably be something like "da." If the adults who hear this sound immediately squeal with delight, laugh, smile, or give affection to the child, these social reinforcers will increase the likelihood that the baby will repeat this sound. This and other sounds will be reinforced, and the likelihood of their occurring again will thereby be strengthened. In this way, random noises begin to grow into words. The child is reinforced for his baby talk until he is ready for more articulate sounds. The adults will then hold back praise or not give any praise until the child makes more articulate sounds. The baby talk is thus gradually extinguished and soon, through positive reinforcement, sounds like "da" will emerge as "dad" or "daddy." Because adult speech is built on the child's early undifferentiated sounds, the child who never received praise or any other reinforcement for his baby talk most likely would not have learned to talk at all. Through the shaping process, the child builds sounds into words and, later, words into sentences.

The behavioral psychology laboratory has provided us with much interesting evidence of the process of shaping. In the laboratories pigeons, rats, and other animals have been trained to perform many new complex behaviors.

STUDY QUESTIONS: SHAPING BEHAVIOR

1. Check the statements below that are true:

☐ **a.** Behavior is made up of unconnected units.

☐ **b.** A desired behavior can be developed in stages.

☐ **c.** New behaviors can be developed through training.

☐ **d.** Shaping is a gradual, training process.

☐ **e.** Shaping implies that, at first, behavior which is not completely correct is built up in small steps and strengthened until the desired behavior is reached.

2. Name at least three ways to reinforce a baby when shaping his verbal behavior from baby talk to adult speech.

a.

b.

c.

The following description of training sessions with a pigeon will show you how the shaping process is carried out in the laboratory.

> Pecking is a behavior which is natural to pigeons. However, pigeons do not peck in a particular area. The objective in the laboratory has been to teach the pigeon to peck in a circle drawn on one of the walls of a special training box. The circle is placed approximately at the eye level of the pigeon. Eventually the pigeon will receive food only when he pecks the circle, but since pecking within a circle is not part of a pigeon's natural behavior, it must be taught to the pigeon through the process of shaping.
>
> The following is a description of the shaping process: When the pigeon is first placed in the experimental box, he responds in a variety of ways: he pecks the floor and walls of the box; he flaps his wings; he walks in circles around the box. The pigeon's most important response is pecking, and this is the response that will be shaped into pecking in a circle. The reinforcement for the pigeon is food. At first, the pigeon will be given food anytime he pecks, regardless of where or what he pecks. Other behavior, such as wing flapping and walking around the experimental box, will not be reinforced; that is, the pigeon will not receive food for behaving in these ways. The pigeon will soon stop all wing flapping and other extraneous behavior except pecking. These nonreinforced behaviors will gradually extinguish.
>
> The pigeon's head-lifting behavior must be strengthened before the pigeon can even locate the circle. Therefore, the next step after strengthening the pigeon's random pecking behavior is to give him food immediately after he lifts his head. Later, the pigeon must lift his head and then peck in order to receive food. Gradually the psychologist will raise the standards for head lifting and pecking and will not reward the pigeon with food until the pigeon lifts his head to full height, and then pecks. This response will bring the pigeon to the correct height so that he will stop pecking on the floor and will be more likely to locate the circle, at the same time extinguishing the behavior of pecking on the floor. Note that in this process of shaping, the pigeon gets

reinforced for behavior that comes closer and closer to the final desired behavior. Once he reaches a certain level of performance, the requirements are increased and he no longer receives a reward for his earlier behavior.

Let's retrace the steps in the shaping process thus far:

1. First the pigeon is rewarded for pecking anything at all.
2. Then he is rewarded for lifting his head a little and pecking.
3. At appropriate levels, he is rewarded for the gradual lifting of his head to its full height (eye level) and then pecking.

Once head lifting to the proper height is sufficiently strengthened, the psychologist will no longer reward this behavior. He will wait for the pigeon to peck the wall on which the circle is found. Once the pigeon pecks this particular wall, he will get fed. Now the pigeon no longer receives food simply for lifting his head and pecking, but only for pecking the wall with the circle on it. At some point the pigeon will happen to peck the wall close to the circle and this response will be reinforced with food. Eventually, the pigeon will peck the circle itself and this response will finally be the *only* one that will be reinforced.

Thus, during the process of shaping, the learner (a pigeon) receives reinforcement (food) for responses that come closer and closer to some behavioral objective (pecking a circle). As the learner demonstrates that he is able to perform successfully at one stage in his training, he no longer will receive reinforcement for these responses, and these responses will extinguish. The shaping process for responses that come increasingly closer to the final, desired response continues until the learner acquires the new behavior. If the teacher (in this case, the behavioral psychologist) had from the beginning rewarded the learner (the pigeon) only when he pecked the circle and had never shaped the other preliminary responses (at first, all pecking responses, then head raising, pecking the wall with the circle on it, and so on), the pigeon would never have learned to peck the circle.

A student's new behavior may be shaped using the similar procedure of reinforcement at each stage of the learning process. As the student reaches some particular level of success, his teacher then can raise the standards and reinforce him for performing a task that is slightly more difficult, or for performing the same task slightly better than he has done it in the past. In this way he will gradually acquire new skills.

The process of shaping can be seen also in the training of a high jumper in track. At first the bar is set very low, at a point where the jumper can clear it easily. Gradually the bar is raised. The reinforcement is a successful clearing of the bar. Each time the bar is raised, the criterion for a reinforcement (a successful jump), is also raised. In this way the jumper can be trained to clear the bar, and to strive gradually toward making a higher and higher jump.

Answer the following questions to see how well you understand the process of shaping behavior.

3. The following is a list of the preliminary behaviors which were reinforced in the process of shaping a pigeon's behavior to peck a circle. Number them in the sequence in which you would reinforce them in order to arrive at the final behavior.

a. ______ lifting his head to full height (eye level), then pecking

b. ______ lifting the head and then pecking

c. ______ pecking anything

d. ______ pecking close to the circle

e. ______ pecking the wall with the circle on it

f. ______ pecking the circle

4. a. How was the behavior of the high jumper in track shaped?

b. What was the reward or reinforcement for this behavior?

SHAPING AND TEACHING

How do we bring about desirable behavior in the classroom? Teaching is the process of shaping new behavior, first by providing the necessary information and activities, and then by reinforcing the appropriate behavior. Once you, the instructor, have denied the behavioral objectives that are reasonable for each student, you are ready to shape his behavior, keeping in mind that the shaping process takes place at different rates for each student. Some students acquire new skills more slowly and with greater difficulty; some need more demonstrations; others need more practice; some learn better when they work with a partner; others work better alone; still another student might require more frequent praise even though his work is not perfect. The teacher has the challenging task of identifying each student's learning process and learning rate carefully so that every individual in the class will acquire the skills most efficiently and will perform at his best level. Each student must be given the opportunity to reach some level of success so that he can build his future responses upon his past behavior.

SHAPING A NEW BEHAVIOR TO REPLACE AN OLD BEHAVIOR

The shaping process suggests that behavior is the result of a continuous series of responses or actions. Some of these responses will not be reinforced and thereafter will be less likely to occur and will eventually extinguish. Some responses will be reinforced and therefore will be more likely to occur. In this way some final behavior will be reached. Once a new behavior is established it needs only occasional reinforcement for that response to become permanent.

SUMMARY

Old behavior patterns can be extinguished while new behaviors are being shaped to replace the old behavior. The new behavior is said to compete with the old behavior; that is, the only behavior that will bring a reinforcement is the new response, not the old response.

Let's see how competing behaviors are shaped in a classroom situation.

> You, an instructor, have a student who calls out to you from his seat to ask questions and usually interrupts you and the class.

If you answer him so that you can go on with your point, you are strengthening the calling-out and interrupting behavior. In order to shape new behavior, you must allow the old behavior to extinguish by removing the reinforcements—by not answering him. Ignoring him denies the student your attention and also prevents him from getting his question answered. Eventually this attention-getting behavior should extinguish. (The trick here is for you to have the patience to wait out the extinction period without further reinforcing the behavior by giving him added attention such as lecturing him in front of the class, because this kind of attention is often exactly what the student is seeking.)

Instead of this negative attention-getting behavior, you want to set up competing, desired behavior which will bring on the reward of your attention and praise. Getting the student to raise his hand or come up to your desk when you have finished giving directions to the class is a more desirable response. In order to shape these responses, you must inform the student of the alternative responses that will be acceptable to you. However, telling him what you expect is not sufficient to shape new behavior. Some students may, it is true, respond to your telling them how to behave differently; but many students will require a longer shaping period. You must first wait for the student to do something that is an improvement over the calling-out behavior, even if it is not the behavior you consider the most desirable. If, for example, your student raises his hand before calling out his question, you might answer him at that time. Although he has not given you a chance to call on him, first raising his hand represents an improvement over mere calling out. Eventually, you will recognize him only when he raises his hand, and only when he does not interrupt you. You will also have to set up other more acceptable ways for the student to get attention rather than by calling out in class.

Consider other examples, such as the student who sets low standards for himself by doing incomplete or messy work, or the one who has a negative attitude toward school and doesn't participate in class. These students often receive negative reinforcements, such as failing grades, stern lectures, words and looks of displeasure from their teachers, that serve only to strengthen the students' negative attitude and their dislike for learning. Such students must be given every opportunity to succeed and receive praise, no matter how hard the teacher has to look to find some little thing the student can do well. Every slight improvement must be recognized. When a failing student gets a "D," rather than an "F," he deserves praise because he has improved. If on one examination, a student gets nine out of ten questions incorrect and on a later examination, he gets only six out of ten incorrect, he deserves some recognition for his improvement. Very gradually such a student can build on his past successes rather than upon his past failures. The fundamental notion of shaping desired behavior depends upon the principle of positive reinforcement given for responses that come closer and closer to some final desired behavior.

5. Shaping a student's behavior involves the following steps. Number them in the order that they should occur:

a. ______ identifying the desired final response

b. ______ reinforcing any response that approximates the desired response

c. ______ reinforcing only the desired response

d. ______ reinforcing the response that comes closer and closer to the desired response

6. In the essay on defining behavior you read about the problem of getting the patients in a mental hospital to behave in a more desirable way and to arrive in the dining room in less time. Refer back to this essay, if you wish. Match the procedure in the left column with the actual situation in the right column.

a. setting initial standards	1.	______	all patients getting to the dining room 5 minutes after the dinner bell is rung
b. gradually raising standards	2.	______	all patients walking to the dining room without the need of escorts
c. reinforcement	3.	______	closing the dining room door 20 minutes after the dinner bell is rung
d. arriving at the final desired behavior	4.	______	closing the dining room door 10 minutes after the dinner bell is rung
	5.	______	getting fed

7. Judy wants to learn to ride a two-wheel bike. What behavior would you shape first? second? and so on.

- **a.** ______ riding a two-wheel bike with someone running alongside holding the seat whenever necessary
- **b.** ______ riding a two-wheel bike with no outside support
- **c.** ______ riding a two-wheel bike without guide wheels with someone holding onto the seat
- **d.** ______ riding a three-wheeled bike
- **e.** ______ riding a two-wheel bike with guide wheels on the back

8. A student who has been failing in your course finally does "fair" rather than "poor" work. Should you praise him? Why or why not?

ANSWER KEY

SHAPING BEHAVIOR

1. **b.** a desired behavior can be developed in stages
   c. new behaviors can be developed through training
   d. shaping is a gradual, training process
   e. shaping implies that at first behavior which is not completely correct is built upon and strengthened until the desired behavior is obtained

2. Your response should include any three of the following:
   a. smiling
   b. giving affection
   c. giving attention
   d. saying "That's good," or giving some equivalent praise
   e. feeding him

3. **a.** 3
   b. 2
   c. 1
   d. 5
   e. 4
   f. 6

4. The high jump bar is gradually raised, thereby raising the standard for success. A successful jump is the reward of reinforcement.

5. **a.** 1
   b. 2
   c. 4
   d. 3

6. **1.** D
   2. D
   3. A
   4. B
   5. C

7. a. 4
   b. 5
   c. 3
   d. 1
   e. 2

8. Yes, you should praise him, for you want to strengthen this improved behavior. Using positive reinforcement is the best way to assure this increase on the part of the student. For example, you might say that you've noticed he has improved. You might provide opportunities for him to do very good work by giving him easier tasks which you are certain that he can do.

A PROGRAMMED INSTRUCTION COURSE

In the unit that follows, try to answer correctly before looking at the response given. Use a piece of cardboard as a mask. Beginning at the top of the frame, slide the mask down until you come to a light horizontal rule. Read the frame and answer the question. Then slide the mask down to uncover the answer and see if you were correct. Some frames contain more than one question; therefore, you should uncover one line at a time until all questions have been answered and a new frame has begun.

I

INTRODUCTION TO PROGRAMMED INSTRUCTION

NOW SLIDE THE MASK DOWN TO THE RULE, AND STOP

Programmed instruction is different from ordinary classroom or textbook instruction. In a program, you are presented with some information and then asked to answer one or more questions about the information.

Read the following sentence. Then check the correct choice in the question that follows:

Cornell University

☐ is like a high school. ☐ is like a college.

NOW CHECK YOUR ANSWER WITH THE ONE BELOW

---

is like a college.

II

NOW SLIDE THE MASK

Sometimes you will be required to check only one box as you did in the question you just answered and sometimes you will have to check **more than** one box.

For example, check each choice below that describes a facility at a small college or high school.

☐ beauty parlor ☐ sauna bath
☐ dormitories ☐ laboratories
☐ classrooms

NOW CHECK YOUR ANSWER

---

dormitories, classrooms, laboratories

III

NOW SLIDE THE MASK

REFER BACK TO FRAMES I AND II

When you work in a program, you often answer questions with several choices. You may be required to

☐ check only one choice in a list of choices.

☐ check more than one choice in a list of choices.

NOW CHECK YOUR ANSWER

Both answers should be checked.

IV

NOW SLIDE THE MASK

Blocks of information and questions are numbered consecutively. In programmed instruction, each block is called a **frame.**

The frame you are now reading is Frame IV.

Look back at Frames I and II. In which frames(s) was (were) there more than one choice?

☐ Frame I

☐ Frame II

NOW CHECK YOUR ANSWER

Frame II

V

NOW SLIDE THE MASK

Sometimes you will be asked to fill in a blank. You may have to write a word, a phrase, a sentence, or several sentences.

Try this one:

The name of the course I am taking is

NOW CHECK YOUR ANSWER

(You should have written the name of the course you are taking in the space provided.)

VI

NOW SLIDE THE MASK

Most frames are like the ones you have just read.

In a frame, you

1. read information.
2. answer a question or several questions.
3. check your answers with the answers given.

Compared to learning from a textbook, programmed instruction is different because:

☐ a program requires the student to read information only.

☐ a program requires the student to answer questions about the information he reads.

NOW CHECK YOUR ANSWER

---

a program requires the student to answer questions about the information he reads.

SLIDE THE MASK

After answering a question in a frame of a program, you check your answer by

☐ asking a teacher if you are correct.

☐ having someone else correct your answers.

☐ sliding down the mask and comparing your own answers with the ones below the light horizontal rule.

NOW CHECK YOUR ANSWER

---

sliding down the mask and comparing your own answers with the ones below the light horizontal rule.

VII

Check the phrase that correctly completes the following sentence:

The sliding mask is used to cover the correct answers so that you

☐ will write your own answer before you see the correct answer.

☐ can see the correct answer before you have written your own answer.

---

will write your own answer before you see the correct answer.

VIII

When you have completed the last question on a page, turn to the next page and slide the mask down to the rule immediately, so that it completely covers the answer below it.

This procedure is recommended to make sure that, as you turn to the next page, you

- ☐ will see the correct answer(s) on that page before you answer the question(s).
- ☐ will not see the correct answer(s) on that page until you have answered the question(s).

---

will not see the correct answer(s) on that page until you have answered the question(s).

IX

There are several other things you should know about learning from a program.

You may be asked to match items from one column with items in another column. For example, look at the following matching problem and examine how it is answered.

Match the following:

A. served in the French and Indian War	1. ______ George Washington
B. was president of the United States of America	2. ______ Dwight D. Eisenhower
C. attended the U.S. Military Academy at West Point	
D. resided at estate in Mount Vernon, Virginia	

---

1. A, B, D 2. B, C

You can see that matching questions may have

☐ only one letter placed in a blank.

☐ more than one letter placed in a blank.

---

more than one letter placed in a blank.

Was (were) there any item(s) that matched with both George Washington and Dwight D. Eisenhower?

☐ yes ☐ no

---

yes

If yes, which item(s)?

☐ A ☐ B ☐ C ☐ D

B

X

When you answer a matching question, you take the letters of the items in the left hand column and write them in the appropriate blank in the right hand column.

Try this one.

Match the following:

A. Augusta	1. ______ states
B. Connecticut	2. ______ capitals
C. Denver	
D. Florida	
E. Ohio	

1. B, D, E   2. A, C

XI

Often you are asked to read an example.

Instead of including a long example within a frame, you may be asked to look at a separate case inserted in the program.

You only use the case when you see an instruction like:

TURN TO CASE A
or
REFER TO CASE B

No response required; go on to the next Frame.

XII

TURN FORWARD TO CASE A (p. 64)

The instruction above tells you to use Case A.

Now answer the following questions.

Case A describes

☐ an example of a student behavior problem.

☐ an explanation of ways to teach home economics.

☐ a suggestion for lesson planning.

an example of a student behavior problem.

In order to answer the above questions you were supposed to

☐ read the case. ☐ make a guess.

---

read the case.

XIII

You should always turn to the appropriate frame when there is an instruction like:

TURN TO FRAME 1
or
REFER TO FRAME 3

You will not be able to learn from answering questions unless you use all of the information to which you are referred.

From the above, you can tell that in order to work through a program successfully you should

☐ follow the instructions in a program.

☐ read only the instructions you think are important.

☐ read carefully all of the information provided in each frame.

---

follow the instructions in a program.

read carefully all of the information provided in each frame.

Some information you will learn in a program will be found

☐ in the frame on which you are presently working.

☐ in previous frames that you have completed.

☐ in a separate case.

All answers should be checked.

XIV

Now let's review.

You know that, while taking this program, you may be required to

- ☐ check one item.
- ☐ check two or more items.
- ☐ check all items.
- ☐ fill in a blank with one or more words or numbers.
- ☐ match several items.
- ☐ refer to a case.

All answers should be checked.

XV

In addition to providing information, and an opportunity for you to answer questions and check your answers, an important feature of a program is that it lets you learn at your own pace. Results obtained using programs show that successful learning does not depend upon how long it takes you to finish the program.

Thus, you should

- ☐ move along at a fairly fast rate.
- ☐ move along at a fairly slow rate.
- ☐ move along at your own best rate.
- ☐ try to compete with the rates of others.

---

move along at your own best rate.

XVI

As you take this program, your pace will be

- ☐ set by an instructor who tells you when to go on to the next frame.
- ☐ determined by you at whatever pace is most comfortable.

---

determined by you at whatever pace is most comfortable.

XVII

The frames in a program present information in an easy to understand, step-by-step fashion. Each frame builds on the ones before, so that you gradually learn more and more about the subject you are studying.

As a result, when the questions become harder later in the program, you are prepared for them and will find that you will be able to answer them without difficulty.

Thus, you

- ☐ probably will not be able to answer many of the questions.
- ☐ should be able to answer nearly all the questions correctly.
- ☐ should expect to make many errors as you work through the program.

---

should be able to answer nearly all the questions correctly.

XVIII

PREVIEW FRAME

REMEMBER! No matter what kind of answer you are called upon to make, it is always important to check your answer against the one in the correct response box; **and** follow these rules:

Don't skip pages.

Always write in your answer.

If your answer is incorrect, read the frame again and try to understand it before you go on. This is the only time you should look back.

Follow instructions about panels as you come to them.

Now that you know how to use a self-instructional program, you will begin to study the process of behavior change.

No response required; go on to Frame 1.

1

INTRODUCTORY FRAME

You, as a teacher, have the opportunity to create conditions in your classroom to help each student learn the most effectively and to respond to you and his classmates the most favorably. It is likely that most of your students function well. You can ascertain that they are acquiring new skills and learning new concepts, and you can observe them working cooperatively with you and with their classmates, and adhering to the class rules and school procedures.

However, there may be a few students who behave in a way that hinders or prevents them from performing as well as they are capable, or students whose actions tend to create friction or tension in the class. How would you go about helping these students behave in a more desirable way?

You are about to learn a process for identifying undesirable behavior and bringing about more desirable behavior in such students.

No response required; go on to the next Frame.

Before you can begin to change the way a student is behaving, you must ask yourself, "What is the student doing **now** that I find undesirable?"

Mr. Anderson has a few students in his class whose behavior he describes in this way:

> Jack is very talkative in class and he does not complete his classwork. Most of his papers are handed in late.
>
> Ralph leaves a job half finished and then begins a new project; leaving the second unfinished, he proceeds to a third.
>
> Sandra works very quickly but her work is usually inaccurate, incomplete, and messy.

In the statements above, what kind of behavior did Mr. Anderson describe?

☐ desirable behavior

☐ undesirable behavior

---

undesirable behavior

Mr. Anderson recognizes that before any behavior can be changed the instructor should first

☐ identify the undesirable behavior.

☐ take some action to change the behavior.

---

identify the undesirable behavior.

3

You will recall that the process of describing the behavior of any student (whether the behavior to be described is desirable or undesirable) involves identifying the student's action.

Which of the following* would most **accurately** describe the undesirable behavior of Bob, a student?

☐ Bob's behavior is a problem.

☐ Bob interrupts me when I am talking to the class.

☐ Bob is difficult to manage in class.

Bob interrupts me when I am talking to the class.

4

Read the example below.

Sam's assignment in typing class is to type an article for the class newspaper. After he types a few sentences, he takes the paper to his teacher and asks, "Does this look okay?" Then he goes back to his seat, types a few more sentences, and returns to the teacher asking, "Is the spacing all right?" Again he returns to his seat but soon goes up to the teacher for the third time with still another question.

Miss Carter, the typing instructor, was overheard saying to a colleague in the staff room, "Sam Post really gets on my nerves!" Her colleague asked, "Just what is Sam doing that 'gets on your nerves'?"

*If you had difficulty answering this question or if you wish to review the concepts of how to describe behavior, you may wish to refer back to the paragraphs on defining and describing behavior in the chapter "Principles of Behavior Theory."

In answering her colleague, which of the following statements would best identify specifically what Sam was doing that was undesirable?

- ☐ raising his hand and asking questions
- ☐ bringing his work up too frequently to Miss Carter to have her check it
- ☐ completing his work before showing it to Miss Carter
- ☐ getting on Miss Carter's nerves

---

bringing his work up too frequently to Miss Carter to have her check it

5

Paul is a very enthusiastic student. He eagerly completes all his assignments and works industriously in class. He follows direction independently and completes most projects accurately. At the end of the period, Paul leaves scraps on the floor of the room and his tools out on his work table.

In your own words, describe Paul's undesirable behavior.

Paul leaves the room without cleaning up his work area. (Obviously, you may use your own wording in any questions of this type.)

6

Once you have identified the undesirable student behavior, you should consider what you would like to have the student do instead.

For example:

If you have a student who spends much of his class time "daydreaming" (staring off into space, not working), you should decide how you would rather see this student behave.

Read the statements below:

1. The student should learn to behave in class.
2. The student should learn to pay attention to a given task for a longer period of time.
3. The student should learn to stop daydreaming.

Which statement above best describes the behavior that would be most desirable?

☐ 1

☐ 2

☐ 3

2

7

Mrs. Johnson had a student, Ted, who kept coming up to her desk to have his work checked. As soon as the student had completed one small part of his project, he would ask whether or not his work was satisfactory.

Mrs. Johnson felt that Ted demanded too much attention. She considered the following alternative behaviors:

1. Ted should begin to develop the skill of evaluating his own work so that he does not have to rely on his teacher's approval all the time.
2. Ted should complete at least a section of a project before he brings his work up for approval.
3. Ted should stop seeking attention.
4. Ted should work completely by himself until the end of the period, when he should hand in a completed assignment.

Which choice(s) above do you think best identifies (identify) the preferred way (ways) Ted should behave?

☐ 1

☐ 2

☐ 3

☐ 4

1, 2

8

You have a student whose behavior you would like to change. You have identified the undesirable behavior and you have also defined how you would like the student to behave instead. Match the undesirable behavior (in the column on the left) with the appropriate desirable behavior that should replace it (in the column on the right).

A. interrupting the teacher	1. ______	cleaning up before leaving the classroom
B. socializing too much with classmates	2. ______	waiting to be called upon before speaking in class discussion
C. leaving tools on work table	3. ______	working on his class work independently
	4. ______	working on class assignments, concentrating on the task at hand

---

1. C   2. A   3. B   4. B

9

You have identified the behavior of one of your students, Paul, as undesirable: he has left scraps on the floor of the room and tools on his work table.

In your own words, describe the way you would like to have Paul behave instead.

Paul should clean his work area before leaving the room and he should put tools away in their proper places.

10

Bob is a very enthusiastic student. He is always ready to answer any question you ask the class. However, he calls out an answer before you can call on other students. Consequently, few of the other class members have an opportunity to participate. What is undesirable about Bob's behavior that you want to change?

Bob calls out the answers before being called upon and before he raises his hand.

What behavior might you want to occur instead of this behavior?

Have Bob raise his hand and/or wait to be called upon.

11

The first step the instructor took in changing Bob's behavior (referred to in the previous frame) was to

☐ try to identify the undesirable behavior that was occurring.

☐ try to stop Bob from behaving in an undesirable way.

---

try to identify the undesirable behavior that was occurring.

12

The first step in the behavior process involves two identifications. You first identify the student's undesirable behavior. What further identification should you make before you proceed to change his behavior?

- ☐ You should identify the method of changing the undesirable behavior.
- ☐ You should identify the behavior that you consider more desirable and that should replace the undesirable behavior.
- ☐ You should identify ways to prevent the student from behaving in an undesirable way.

You should identify the behavior that you consider more desirable and that should replace the undesirable behavior.

13

The first step in the process of changing a student's behavior is for the instructor to make **two** identifications.

Check the correct choices below.

The instructor should

- ☐ identify the action he should take to change the student's behavior.
- ☐ identify the desirable behavior that should take place.
- ☐ identify the undesirable behavior that is occurring.

---

identify the desirable behavior that should take place.

identify the undesirable behavior that is occurring.

14

You have a student whose behavior is in some way undesirable. If you want to change this behavior, what must you **identify first** before you can proceed to bring about new behavior?

and

Your answer should include the following parts:

Identify the undesirable behavior

and

identify the desirable behavior you would like to have occur instead.

CASE A

In Mrs. Grant's Home Economics class, the girls are frequently divided into small working groups. For one of the projects, each group was to plan a menu and cook and serve a dinner to the class. The members of each group were instructed to share their ideas, formulate plans, and divide the various tasks among themselves. Most of the groups worked well together, except for one. Mrs. Grant noticed that in this group, Claudia really took over the group and none of the other girls was able to voice her opinion. Mrs. Grant observed the ill feeling and bad temper of the group and that the group could not agree on anything. She decided to discuss the situation with Claudia after class.

Mrs. Grant: Claudia, how do you think the plans in your group are coming along?

Claudia: Oh, I'm really fed up. The girls in my group don't have any good ideas and we never get anything done in class.

Mrs. Grant: Why do you think you are having so much trouble in your group?

Claudia: They just can't make up their minds and when I try to make suggestions they don't ever want to listen.

Mrs. Grant: I'm really glad to see that you are so enthusiastic about the coming project. Are you aware that because you are so excited about your own ideas the other girls in your group don't have a chance to share theirs and perhaps they resent your taking over the group?

Claudia: Gee, I didn't think it was so bad. It seems to me that the others don't care and anyhow, they don't seem to know how to do anything right. I thought I was helping them out.

Mrs. Grant: I believe you can share your enthusiasm and use your leadership ability more effectively. Do you have any ideas as to how to go about it?

Claudia: Not really. I guess I get carried away. I didn't realize I was bossing the other girls around.

CASE A

Conclusion 1

Mrs. Grant: I have an idea. Why not volunteer to be secretary of your group? Your role will be to organize their ideas. You will have to try hard to get everyone to offer some suggestion for the menu. Maybe this way everyone will participate in the planning. Then, after you have all the ideas, you can each volunteer to do that part of the project you would most enjoy. How does that sound?

Claudia: Pretty good. I'd be willing to try it.

Mrs Grant: Good. I'm glad we talked about this. If you find that this method doesn't work, come back and we'll try something else.

Conclusion 2

Mrs Grant:	Let's see whether the group has any ideas as to how to go about the project. (Mrs. Grant calls the group together.) How do you girls think your project is coming along?
Gloria:	We weren't getting anything done.
Sue:	That's right. No one wants to do anything.
Mrs Grant:	What is the real problem?
Nancy:	I don't mean to be blunt, but Claudia, you never let us have a say in any of the plans. I guess no one wants you to tell us what to do. (The other girls nod in agreement.)
Mrs Grant:	What do you think is the best way to change this situation?
Nancy:	Claudia really has great ideas, but I'd like to put in my two cents' worth even if my ideas aren't so good; and I'm sure Sue and Gloria would, too.
Sue:	Well, I have one idea. If we can use the blackboard, maybe we could all write out a menu on the board and then we'd all have a chance to read each other's. Then maybe we could try to take at least one idea from each menu.
Claudia:	That's a good idea, Sue. I didn't know I was being such a boss.
Mrs Grant:	Claudia, it seems as though your group feels you have good ideas. It's just that each girl wants to play some part. Besides cooking, there are other jobs, like writing out the menus, table setting, and so on. I'll help you develop a list of these details and each of you can sign up next to the jobs you would like to do.
All the girls:	Thank you, Mrs. Grant.

15

When a teacher is faced with a student who behaves in some undesirable way, the teacher should not try to solve the problem alone. He has other resources available to him. One of the most important people who can help the teacher work out a solution is the student himself. Once you, the teacher, have identified a student's behavior as a problem and you have determined the behavior that you would like to occur instead, you may have a conference with the student and ask him about his behavior. The student may or may not recognize that he is behaving in an undesirable way and he may or may not have suggestions as to how to change his behavior. However, unless you involve him in a discussion of the problem, you will not know whether he is aware of his undesirable behavior.

TURN TO CASE A

What behavior had Mrs. Grant identified as undesirable?

- ☐ Claudia's enthusiasm
- ☐ Claudia's talking out of turn in class
- ☐ Claudia's uncooperative group behavior

Claudia's uncooperative group behavior

How did Mrs. Grant learn whether or not Claudia recognized her own undesirable behavior?

- ☐ Mrs. Grant first asked Claudia to describe the problem from Claudia's point of view.
- ☐ Mrs. Grant immediately explained what her own objections were to Claudia's behavior.

Mrs. Grant first asked Claudia to describe the problem from Claudia's point of view.

REFER TO CASE A

What behavior did Mrs. Grant want to change?

Claudia's overpowering leadership or her inability to allow her classmates to share their ideas and work cooperatively as a group

What did Mrs. Grant want to help Claudia do?

She told her to cooperate more effectively; allow other students to participate.

How did Mrs. Grant make Claudia aware of her undesirable behavior and thereby involve her student in the behavior change process?

She held a conference with her (discussed her behavior with her).

17

Once you have identified the behavior to be changed and you have determined what behavior you want to strengthen, how can you make the student aware of his undesirable behavior?

Discuss the student's behavior with him.

18

REVIEW FRAME

You have now completed the **first** step in the process of behavior change.

You have:

identified the undesirable behavior.

identified the desirable behavior you would like to occur instead.

discussed the student's behavior with him.

Now you are ready to begin step 2 in the process of bringing about the desirable behavior and eliminating the undesirable behavior: **making** your own suggestions for changing the behavior and **getting** suggestions from the student himself and **consulting** other sources, such as psychological and guidance resource people.

No response required; go on to the next Frame.

19

REFER TO CASE A

When Claduia was asked to describe her behavior, Mrs. Grant learned that Claudia

☐ was aware of the fact that she was uncooperative.

☐ was not aware of the fact that she was uncooperative.

---

was not aware of the fact that she was uncooperative.

20

REFER TO CASE A

From the example in Case A, you can conclude that when you hold a discussion with a student about his behavior you should first

☐ ask him to describe his own behavior to you.

☐ tell him what you think is wrong with his behavior.

---

ask him to describe his own behavior to you.

21

REFER TO CASE A

Once Mrs. Grant learned that Claudia could not describe her problem behavior, Mrs. Grant helped out by explaining to Claudia what was objectionable about the way she was acting in her group.

What did Mrs. Grant tell Claudia?

She told Claudia that she wasn't giving the other girls a chance to share their ideas.

22

REFER TO CASE A: Conclusion 1*

Since Claudia had no suggestions to offer as to how she might work in a more cooperative manner, Mrs. Grant made one.

Mrs. Grant's suggestion for Claudia to be group secretary

- ☐ would enable Claudia to use her leadership skills.
- ☐ would make it more likely that Claudia would continue to be an uncooperative group member.
- ☐ would not provide the opportunity for Claudia to participate in the group.

---

would enable Claudia to use her leadership skills.

23

REFER TO CASE A, Conclusion 1

Who identified Claudia's undesirable behavior?

- ☐ Claudia
- ☐ Mrs. Grant

Mrs. Grant

*Conclusion 2 will be referred to further on in the lesson.

Did Claudia offer any suggestions to help change her own behavior?

☐ yes

☐ no

---

no

In a situation such as the one described in Case A, how did Mrs. Grant help bring about the change in Claudia's behavior?

She made suggestions on how Claudia could improve group relations.

24

When you have a discussion with a student about his behavior, you should try to determine

☐ whether the student is able to recognize his own problem behavior.

☐ whether the student is not able to recognize his own problem behavior.

Both choices should be checked.

25

In which situation described below will the teacher be the more likely to learn how the student views his own behavior?

☐ when the teacher first asks the student to describe his own behavior

☐ when the teacher first explains her objections to the student's behavior

---

when the teacher first asks the student to describe his own behavior

26

If, during a conference with a student, you discover that the student is *not* able to recognize what he is doing that is objectionable, you

☐ should explain to him your own objections to his behavior

☐ should not explain your objections to him

and

☐ should make suggestions about what he might do to improve.

☐ should not make suggestions about what he might do to improve.

---

should explain to him your own objections to his behavior
and
should make suggestions about what he might do to improve.

27

During a discussion with a student about his "problem" behavior, you discover that the student is not able to describe or recognize what is undesirable about his behavior.

What should you tell the student during such a conference?

and

Your answer should include:
You should explain your objections to his behavior
and
you should make suggestions about what the student could do to change his behavior.

CASE B

Mr. Sanford has a student who seems to have a very short attention span. He can't work on a project for long before he has to get up out of his seat to wander around the room. He often ends up by disturbing the other students.

Mr. Sanford has a conference with this student.

Mr. Sanford: Joel, you seem to have difficulty concentrating for very long on a task. You get very little done in class and you end up talking to your classmates and disturbing them as well.

Joel: Mr. Sanford, I know I'm restless but I really need to walk around every so often. I think I might work much better if I didn't have to stay on one project all period, and also if I could take a break and get out of my seat.

Mr. Sanford: I appreciate your request. Let's work out a list of acceptable projects which you can choose to work on. We can make up some kind of work schedule so that you won't just hop from project to project without finishing any of them. When you feel like taking a break, that's fine; but try to avoid disturbing your classmates. It's all right for you to walk around the room, but try not to distract other students from their work.

28

TURN TO CASE B

How did Mr. Sanford handle the conference?

☐ He allowed Joel to offer suggestions first.

☐ He immediately offered suggestions of his own.

He allowed Joel to offer suggestions first.

Whose suggestion(s) did Mr. Sanford rely upon to help bring about the change in Joel's behavior?

☐ Joel's suggestions only

☐ Mr. Sanford's suggestions only

☐ both Joel's and Mr. Sanford's suggestions

---

both Joel's and Mr. Sanford's suggestions

29

REFER TO CASE B

In the case of Joel's inability to concentrate very long on any one activity, it was clear that

☐ Joel was able to identify his undesirable behavior.

☐ Joel was unable to identify his undesirable behavior.

Joel was able to identify his undesirable behavior.

During the conference, how did Mr. Sanford rely upon the student to help change his old behavior and bring about more desirable behavior?

He allowed the student to offer suggestions which might help bring about more desirable behavior.

30

You discover some behavior that you consider undesirable. You discuss the problem with the student and discover that the student recognizes his problem.

How can you get the student himself to participate in the process of bringing about a change in his behavior?

You should try to ask him to suggest possible solutions (that is, ways in which he believes he could change his behavior).

31

REFER BACK TO CASE A, Conclusions 1 and 2

There are many ways of handling the same problem. The two conclusions to Case A indicate different ways of involving Claudia in identifying the desired behavior.

In Case A, Conclusion 1, who played the most important role in offering suggestions about Claudia's behavior?

☐ Claudia herself

☐ Mrs. Grant

☐ the group

Mrs. Grant

In Case A, Conclusion 2, who played the most important role in making suggestions to bring about a change in Claudia's behavior?

☐ Claudia herself

☐ Mrs. Grant

☐ the group

---

the group

32

REFER BACK TO CASE A, Conclusion 2

Which statement(s) below best describes (describe) the way(s) a solution to the problem of Claudia's uncooperative behavior was reached:

- ☐ Mrs. Grant merely told Claudia what was wrong with the way she had been acting.
- ☐ Mrs. Grant offered suggestions to help Claudia behave in a more desirable way.
- ☐ The group criticized Claudia without offering any suggestions to help her behave in a more desirable way.
- ☐ The group offered suggestions to provide an opportunity for Claudia to behave in a more desirable way.

The group offered suggestions to provide an opportunity for Claudia to behave in a more desirable way.

33

Sometimes the behavior of a student is so complex that an instructor feels that he is unable to handle it alone. Even after discussing the behavior with the student, he feels that the behavior is just too difficult to change. Guidance counselors, psychologists and other such experts are available as outside resource people. They can often shed light on the problem, and will work with the instructor and the student to help bring about a new behavior.

Which people can be helpful in making suggestions to resolve a behavior problem?

- ☐ the instructor
- ☐ the student himself
- ☐ the group or class
- ☐ guidance or psychological services

All choices should be checked.

34

When an instructor comes across a student who is behaving in an undesirable way, and he feels that he cannot solve the problem by himself, he should:

☐ ask the group or class to offer suggestions.

☐ continue to solve the problem alone.

☐ decide that the problem is beyond him and try to give it to someone else to handle.

☐ seek outside resource people, such as guidance counselors.

---

ask the group or class to offer suggestions.
seek outside resource people, such as guidance counselors.

35

You have a student who is having difficulty getting along with other members of the class. Frequently, he gets into arguments with you and with his classmates. He displays a negative attitude toward almost any course assignment and toward you. (For example, he makes statements such as "This stuff bores me.") You have had a conference with him and the two of you have not been able to communicate effectively and resolve the problem.

From whom could you obtain further information or suggestions to help you resolve the problem?

and or

Your answer should have at least one of the following:

guidance and psychological services
and/or
the class or group

36

REVIEW FRAME

You have now completed the **second** step in the behavior change process.

You have:

obtained suggestions from the student himself and/or the group as to ways to change the student's behavior.

offered suggestions of your own as to ways to change the student's behavior.

consulted the guidance and psychological services (if necessary).

In steps 1 and 2 you defined a problem and communicated with the student and, if necessary, with professional resource people. These steps are necessary before you can take any active steps to establish the new behavior.

Now you are ready to make one further identification, which you will learn to do in step 3 of the behavior change process: **identifying** what the student is getting out of behaving in the undesirable way.

No response required; go on to the next Frame.

37

PREVIEW FRAME

During the process of changing a student's behavior, the teacher hopes to weaken and eliminate undesirable behavior and to create instead the right conditions to strengthen and maintain desirable behavior. Once you have identified the undesirable behavior, it is helpful to determine what the student is getting out of behaving in this undesirable way.

You will recall from your reading about the principle of reinforcement* that a behavior which is reinforced is more likely to occur. If you can successfully identify what is strengthening (reinforcing) the undesirable behavior, you will be better able to control and remove these strengtheners (reinforcers), thereby weakening and eliminating the old behavior and setting the stage for a new behavior to take its place.

Identifying what is reinforcing student behavior is not always possible. In this section, you will learn to recognize reinforcers for typical student behavior. In a later lesson, you will learn how to proceed to change behavior even when you are unable to identify the reinforcers for the undesirable behavior.

No response required; go on to the next Frame.

*If you wish to review the concepts of positive reinforcement, refer to the chapter "Principles of Behavior Theory."

38

Once you have identified the undesirable behavior, you say to yourself, "From my point of view, the behavior of that student of mine who continually asks foolish questions is undesirable, but just what is the student getting out of acting the way he is? I think that the questions are really unnecessary. What is strengthening his behavior of asking foolish questions?"

The question that you are asking at this stage in the process of behavioral change is, "What is reinforcing the undesirable behavior?"

The behavior of asking foolish questions is:

☐ desirable

☐ undesirable

---

undesirable

What behavior would be more desirable?

---

asking serious quesions,

or

asking questions that really are questions

39

Behavior that is followed by a positive reinforcer continues to occur. Attention is one example of a positive reinforcer that strengthens many different behaviors. Sometimes attention is given at the wrong times, and a behavior that is not desirable is thereby rewarded and strengthened.

For example:

> A child playing by himself in a room with a group of adults is unnoticed and ignored as he plays quietly and constructively. All of a sudden he starts to make noise and otherwise "act up." This behavior attracts the attention of the adults in the room. They look at him. His mother says something like, "Johnny, what's all that noise about?" In other words, he has become the focus of their attention.

At a future time when this child seeks attention in a roomful of adults, how will he be likely to gain this attention?

☐ He will be likely to make noise.

☐ He will be likely to play constructively and quietly by himself.

He will be likely to make noise.

If by asking silly questions, a student continually gets the teacher's attention, he will seek this reinforcement by

☐ ceasing to ask silly questions.

☐ continuing to ask silly questions.

---

continuing to ask silly questions.

40

Let's take the example of the student who keeps asking foolish questions. You, the instructor, have identified the behavior as undesirable because you feel that the student does not "really" have a question and is just asking questions to get attention.

You just said the word "attention," and that's it!

You recall that every time the student asks a silly question, you stop the class and say, "John, that was a stupid question," or "John, stop wasting the class's time." You recall hearing a few classmates snicker each time this happens. You also realize that the class has stopped working in order to listen to your comments about the foolish questions.

One possible reinforcer of the behavior of asking foolish quesions is getting attention.

How had the student, described above, received the attention he was seeking?

Your answer should include at least one of the following:

The teacher made comments about the foolish questions.

The class laughed.

The class stopped working and paid attention to the student.

41

The instructor has now identified attention as the reinforcer for asking foolish questions.

If the instructor continues to make sarcastic remarks each time the student asks foolish questions, the instructor is

- ☐ strengthening the undesirable behavior (the undesirable behavior will be more likely to occur).
- ☐ weakening the undesirable behavior (the undesirable behavior will be less likely to occur).

---

strengthening the undesirable behavior (the undesirable behavior will be more likely to occur).

42

At this stage in the process of behavior change, you are not only asking **what** is reinforcing the undesirable behavior, but also **who** is providing the reinforcement.

Take the case of the student who kept asking foolish questions. Each time, he heard a sarcastic remark or received a lecture for wasting the class's time. What person was giving the student the attention he was seeking?

---

the instructor

You will recall that this student evoked laughter by asking silly questions. Who provided this reinforcement (attention)?

---

the class

43

In the case of the student who asks foolish questions, something other than attention may be strengthening the undesirable behavior.

You will recall that for the duration of the time that the student was receiving a lecture for wasting time, the regular work of the class had, in fact, stopped. Asking foolish questions may very well have been a way for the student to avoid doing classwork.

How could the student avoid doing classwork?

He could ask foolish questions.

Who is reinforcing this behavior?

---

the instructor (by making comments, lecturing, and so on)

44

You have a student in your class who is readily identified as the class comic. You, too, think he is funny; he successfully gets you off the track and, as a result, you are unable to accomplish what you had planned during class.

What might be maintaining (reinforcing or strengthening) this behavior?

Your answer may include one or both:

getting attention (from you and from the rest of the class)

avoiding work

Who is providing some of the reinforcement to the student for being the class comic?

Both the instructor and the class are providing some of the reinforcement.

CASE C

Mr. Lakin is the instructor in an accounting course. He is troubled by one of his students who does not seem to be able to work effectively in class. The student spends much of his time staring blankly into space or getting up for a drink or wandering around the room.

The following is an excerpt from Mr. Lakin's conference with this student.

Mr. Lakin: Jack, you seem to be having trouble concentrating on the problems you have been assigned to do in class. Can you explain why?

Jack: I think the work is too hard for me. Whenever I try, I get the problems wrong anyhow.

Mr. Lakin: You haven't been asking questions so that you could get help on those things you don't understand.

Jack: I just don't get the whole thing. Besides, when I asked a question last time, you told me that if I had paid attention, I would not have had to ask the question.

45

REFER TO CASE C

Read the discussion between Mr. Lakin and one of his students.

Mr. Lakin's comment, "If you had paid attention, you would have known the answer to that question," is a good example of a negative reinforcer (or punishment).

Jack could eliminate a scolding (that is, he could remove the negative reinforcer) if he

☐ continued to ask questions.

☐ avoided asking any questions.

---

avoided asking any questions.

By providing a negative reinforcer, Mr. Lakin was actually strengthening

☐ desirable behavior.

☐ undesirable behavior.

---

undesirable behavior.

46

REFER TO CASE C

For Jack, performing the accounting problems brought only failure.

Success and failure are measured only after a student actually performs. By not performing, a student's work cannot be evaluated.

In order to avoid failure, Jack decided

☐ to do the accounting problems.

☐ not to do the accounting problems.

---

not to do the accounting problems.

47

REFER TO CASE C

In this case, behavior that is being strengthened is

☐ desirable behavior: asking questions.

☐ undesirable behavior: not asking questions.

---

undesirable behavior: not asking questions.

Why?

By not asking questions, Jack avoids being told that he should have paid attention.

Which behavior is evidently more rewarding to Jack?

☐ doing the accounting problems

☐ not doing the accounting problems

---

not doing the accounting problems

Why?

By not doing the accounting problems, Jack avoids failing.

48

REFER TO CASE C

If a student like Jack keeps failing at a given task he is likely to

☐ continue trying and working hard at the task.

☐ give up and not do the work at all.

---

give up and not do the work at all.

49

REFER TO CASE C

Who was reinforcing Jack's behavior of "not asking questions"?

---

the instructor

How?

---

by reprimanding the student for not paying attention when he was asked a question

50

When you ask yourself the question, What is reinforcing a student's undesirable behavior?, which question below are you really asking?

☐ "What is the desirable behavior that should replace the un-undesirable behavior?"

☐ "What is the undesirable behavior that is occurring at this time?"

☐ "What is the student getting out of behaving in this undesirable way?"

"What is the student getting out of behaving in this undesirable way?"

51

The following presents a review of the first three steps in the behavior change process. Put the steps in the proper order:

_______ **Identify** what the student is getting out of behaving in his undesirable way (**identify** what is reinforcing or strengthening the undesirable behavior).

_______ **Identify** the undesirable behavior. **Identify** the desirable behavior and hold a conference with the student to make him aware of his problem behavior.

_______ **Get** suggestions for a way to change the student's behavior from him or from the class; **consult** outside resource people or make your own suggestions about changing his behavior.

3, 1, 2

52

You have identified some undesirable behavior, and you have also determined what behavior you would like to occur instead and you have discussed the problem with the student (step 1). You have offered suggestions to help the student change his behavior and you have obtained suggestions from him as to ways he might improve his behavior. What should you try to identify next before you can change the undesirable behavior to something more desirable?

Try to identify what the student is getting out of behaving in this undesirable way, and who or what is strengthening and reinforcing this undesirable behavior.

53
REVIEW FRAME

You have now completed the **third** step of the behavior change process.

You have:

identified the reinforcer for the undesirable behavior (whenever possible).

You are now ready to move on to step 4, in which you will take action to **weaken** and **eliminate** the undesirable behavior, and **decide** how to bring about the new behavior in its place.

No response required; go on to the next Frame.

54
PREVIEW FRAME

Once you have identified the reinforcer for some undesirable behavior, the most effective way to weaken the behavior is to **withhold** the reinforcer. This is the process known as extinction.* At the same time that the old behavior is being extinguished, the new behavior can be strengthened. In the frames that follow you will learn the process of weakening or extinguishing undesirable behavior, and the first steps in the process of strengthening new behavior in place of the old behavior.

No response required; go on to the next Frame.

*If you wish to review the concept of extinction, you may refer back to the chapter called "Principles of Behavior Theory."

55

You will recall the example of the pigeon who was trained to peck within a circle. (See the paragraphs on shaping behavior in the chapter called "Principles of Behavior Theory." The pigeon was rewarded with food each time he responded correctly. If the psychologist had wished to extinguish the behavior of pecking the circle, he would after each peck have refrained from giving the pigeon food, and eventually the pigeon would have stopped pecking the circle. That is, the circle-pecking behavior would eventually have become extinguished.

During the process of extinction, reinforcement is

☐ provided.

☐ withheld.

---

withheld.

56

Once an instructor has identified the reinforcer for some undesirable student behavior, this behavior can be extinguished if the reinforcers that are strengthening it are withheld.

For example, attention is often a reinforcer for some undesirable behavior. One effective way to withhold this reinforcer is to ignore the behavior. The act of ignoring is the act of *not* providing (withholding) attention.

If a student makes a wisecrack in class, he is most likely doing it to get attention. One way to withhold the reinforcer is to

☐ continue with the class activity as though nothing had been said.

☐ laugh at him.

☐ say, "Frank, I won't stand for any of that nonsense."

---

continue with the class activity as though nothing had been said.

57

If the behavior of making wisecracks has been previously reinforced because it brought attention to the student, and if the student is now ignored for behaving in this same way, this undesirable behavior

☐ will be less likely to continue.

☐ will be more likely to continue.

---

will be less likely to continue.

58

You have identified a behavior as undesirable, and you would like to extinguish it.

You have

identified the undesirable behavior: asking foolish questions.

identified the reinforcer: getting attention.

determined who has provided the reinforcer: the instructor, himself.

Which action below would be the best way for the instructor to withhold the reinforcer?

☐ reprimanding the student each time he asks a foolish question

☐ refraining, for a while, from calling on the student when he raises his hand

---

refraining, for a while, from calling on the student when he raises his hand

FOOTNOTE FRAME

Extinction is probably the most efficient, practical way to permanently eliminate undesirable behavior. Punishment is too often used to stop undesirable behavior. An extreme example of punishment is imprisonment. While in prison, a criminal cannot commit crimes; that is, his undesirable behavior is temporarily stopped. This solution is often necessary to protect society from a criminal's dangerous behavior, but imprisonment does not necessarily weaken or change the prisoner's criminal behavior.

Common punishments used by instructors are: harsh scolding; sending a student out of the room; issuing sarcastic comments; keeping him after school; or doubling his assignments. These may be effective ways to stop a student from behaving undesirably for the moment, but they will not bring about more desirable ways of behaving. Such methods prevent the behavior from occurring only during the time the punishment is being administered, but they do not necessarily eliminate the undesirable behavior. There is no guarantee against the old behavior's recurrence in the future. However, when an undesirable behavior is extinguished rather than punished, the responses are allowed to occur but when they do occur, the undesirable behavior is not reinforced. Eventually, responses that are not reinforced weaken and are eliminated. It is much more effective to weaken undesirable behavior through the process of extinction than merely to prevent its occurrence by the use of punishment.*

No response required; go on to the next Frame.

*Punishment as a means of stopping extreme forms of undesirable student behavior will be referred to later on in this course.

Punishment is often an ineffective means of controlling behavior. Take the example of the student who acts up in class by continually talking out of turn, telling jokes, or distracting other students. If the instructor had decided to punish the student by yelling at him, sending him out of the room, or keeping him after school, he might have been providing this student with the very attention he was seeking.

Which of the statements below are true?

- ☐ Although punishments such as the ones described above might make some students stop acting up in class, punishing the student doesn't teach him how to behave instead.
- ☐ Behavior may be changed using methods other than punishment.
- ☐ Punishment is the most effective way to weaken undesirable behavior.
- ☐ Punishment may temporarily stop undesirable behavior but will not change the behavior pattern.
- ☐ Punishment should always be used to stop behavior from occurring.
- ☐ Undesirable behavior is best weakened when the reinforcers that strengthen it are withheld.

Although punishments such as the ones described above might make some students stop acting up in class, punishing the student doesn't teach him how to behave instead.

Behavior may be changed using methods other than punishment.

Punishment may temporarily stop undesirable behavior but will not change the behavior pattern.

Undesirable behavior is best weakened when the reinforcers which strengthen it are withheld.

Note: If you did not select all the possible choices, reread Footnote Frame 59.

61

By withholding the reinforcer in the process of changing undesirable behavior, the instructor is

☐ punishing the student.

☐ allowing the undesirable behavior to be extinguished.

---

allowing the undesirable behavior to be extinguished.

62

REFER BACK TO CASE C

Punishing a student not only does not teach a student how to behave, it may also strengthen undesirable behavior.

Take the example of Jack, the student referred to in Case C, who was not doing his accounting problems. The course work was already punishing to him because it resulted in Jack's failure.

If Mr. Lakin, the instructor, had decided that every time Jack did not do his assignment he would punish Jack by doubling his assignment, the punishment would most likely strengthen which of the following behaviors?

☐ Jack might give up altogether.

☐ Jack would do his regular assignment.

☐ Jack would work even harder.

Jack might give up altogether.

63

Once you have begun to weaken the undesirable behavior by **withholding** the reinforcer, you should begin to strengthen a new behavior in its place; but first you must decide what will reinforce or strengthen the new behavior.

Instead of punishing Jack for not doing the accounting problems, Mr. Lakin decided to make accounting a less punishing experience by providing opportunities for Jack to be successful.

Which of the following would be likely ways to provide the necessary reinforcement?

- ☐ Give Jack easier problems to do and praise him for each one he gets correct.
- ☐ Give Jack more problems to do and be critical of the ones he gets incorrect.
- ☐ Give him extra help after class.
- ☐ Provide him with more time to do the classwork.
- ☐ Pair him with a student of his choice who will be able to help him work through the problems.

Give Jack easier problems to do and praise him for each one he gets correct.

Give him extra help after class.

Provide him with more time to do the class work.

Pair him with a student of his choice who will be able to help him work through the problems.

64

You have a student who stands around and doesn't participate in activities. You thought that he was looking for attention, but in reevaluating the problem you decide that this student is really having much difficulty doing many of the tasks required in your course. Your guess is that the student chooses not to do the projects at all and, therefore, stands around idly, rather than attempt the tasks and possibly fail.

Your next step should be to:

- ☐ continue to ignore his standing idle.
- ☐ move the student out of your class.
- ☐ decide to provide some activities which you believe might be easier for him.

---

decide to provide some activities which you believe might be easier for him.

65

The student who has been seeking attention in undesirable ways by acting up in class or by asking foolish questions could get attention in other ways. Therefore, the instructor makes the decision to withhold attention for certain undesirable actions and to instead provide attention for more desirable ways of behaving.

The instructor decides to:

A. provide attention (praise, make a favorable comment)

B. withhold attention (ignore, not say anything)

1. ______ when the student asks a good question
2. ______ when the student makes a foolish remark in class
3. ______ when the student is very conscientious in class

---

1. A 2. B 3. A

You have a student who is consistently late for class. You aren't certain what factors are maintaining this behaivor. However, your guess is that the student arrives late in order to get attention. Which of the following will most likely strengthen the attention-getting behavior?

- ☐ keeping him after school
- ☐ scolding him for being late
- ☐ not saying anything when he enters the room

---

keeping him after school

scolding him for being late

Which of the following will weaken the undesirable attention-getting behavior?

- ☐ keeping him after school
- ☐ giving him a lecture about being on time for class
- ☐ ignoring him

---

ignoring him

Which of the following will strengthen the new behavior of getting to class on time?

- ☐ finding ways for him to get attention or praise in regular class activities
- ☐ ignoring him when he comes to class on time
- ☐ saying, "I'm glad to see you're on time," every time he is not late

---

finding ways for him to get attention or praise in regular class activities

saying, "I'm glad to see you're on time," every time he is not late

67

Once you have identified what is reinforcing undesirable behavior, you then try to **weaken** the undesirable behavior by

☐ withholding the reinforcer of the undesirable behavior.
☐ punishing the student for behaving in an undesirable way.

---

withholding the reinforcer of the undesirable behavior.

68

By withholding the reinforcer, the old behavior will eventually

☐ be strengthened.
☐ be weakened.

---

be weakened.

A new behavior can be strengthened by

☐ withholding the reinforcer.
☐ providing a positive reinforcer.

---

providing a positive reinforcer.

69

In order to change an old behavior, you first identify the reinforcer (whenever possible), and you then withhold the reinforcer for the undesirable behavior. What else must you decide in order to bring about the desirable behavior?

You must decide what reinforcer(s) will strengthen the desirable behavior.

70

Once you have identified what the student is getting out of behaving in an undesirable way (that is, you have—step 3—identified what is reinforcing the undesirable behavior), you are ready to begin the process of weakening the old behavior and strengthening the new behavior.

You can **weaken** the old behavior by **withholding**

---

the reinforcer that is maintaining the undesirable behavior.

Before you can **strengthen** the new behavior you must decide

---

on the reinforcer to strengthen the new behavior.

71

You and one of your students have discussed some undesirable behavior of his and you have identified the reinforcer that is maintaining this old behavior. What should you do at this point to change the old behavior and bring about the new behavior?

and

Withhold the reinforcer that is maintaining the old behavior
and
decide what reinforcer will strengthen the desirable behavior.

72

REVIEW FRAME

In step 3 you **identified** the reinforcer of the undesirable behavior. You now have completed the **fourth** step of the behavior change process.

You have:

withheld the reinforcer for the undesirable behavior.

decided what reinforcer might best **strengthen** the desirable behavior.

Now you are about to learn how to proceed if you are unable to identify the reinforcer of the undesirable behavior.

No response required; go on to the next Frame.

Thus far, you have learned how to begin to change behavior when you have been able to identify the reinforcer. Very often, however, it is difficult to determine just what is keeping an undesirable behavior strong. In a case where you are **unable to identify** the reinforcer for a behavior, you can, nevertheless, create conditions for strengthening a new behavior, one which competes with the old behavior and, therefore, gives the old behavior less chance to occur.

For example: Refer back to Case A (p. 64), the case of Claudia, the uncooperative group member. Her instructor suggested that Claudia be the group secretary.

This suggestion allowed for a competing behavior to "win out" over Claudia's bossiness, because while Claudia was writing down the ideas of other members of her group she would be

- ☐ just as likely to have the opportunity to monopolize the conversation.
- ☐ less likely to have the opportunity to monopolize the conversation.
- ☐ more likely to have the opportunity to monopolize the conversation.

---

less likely to have the opportunity to monopolize the conversation.

CASE D

A professor of an American History course had the habit of pacing back and forth from one side of the room to the other while he gave his lectures. His students found it very distracting to watch him stride back and forth.

One day the professor was late for class and his students had the opportunity to complain to each other about his pacing behavior. They couldn't figure out what made him pace back and forth, but they determined that they would try to make the professor stand still while he lectured.

The students decided on the following plan of action: They chose a spot in the room which they determined would be the lecture spot. They all agreed that they would pay attention to the lecture only when the professor stood at that spot. Paying attention was defined as: looking at the professor, taking notes, asking questions, and looking interested. If the professor paced back and forth or stood anywhere in the room other than the student-designated lecture spot, the students would not pay attention. Not paying attention was defined as: slumping in one's chair, not taking notes, staring out of the window, not asking questions, and looking bored. The students took the process seriously and no one gave the plan away by laughing or exchanging knowing glances.

The first day after the students had formulated their plan, the professor entered the room and began his lecture. As usual, he began pacing back and forth. The whole class immediately began their individual responses indicating not paying attention. As soon as the professor walked to the predetermined spot in the room, they began taking notes, looking interested, and otherwise paying attention. When he moved from this spot, the students again resorted to their nonattentive ways of behaving. The class kept up the process of paying attention only when the professor stood at their chosen lecture spot. At the end of several days of this shaping procedure, the professor's behavior had changed. He stood still, lecturing from the spot the students had selected for him.

74

TURN TO CASE D

Case D describes how a class of students identified some undesirable behavior of their professor and how they changed his behavior.

What behavior did the students want to change?

---

the professor's pacing behavior

What behavior did they want to strengthen instead?

---

the behavior of standing still in one place while lecturing

Before the students could **weaken** the undesirable behavior, what would they have to identify?

The students would have to identify what was reinforcing the pacing behavior.

Before the students could **strengthen** the desirable behavior, what would they have to decide?

The students would have to decide on the reinforcer to strengthen not pacing (or standing still).

CASE E

Mr. Potter teaches a radio and TV repair course. He has a student who seems to give up very quickly when faced with a difficult wiring problem or a challenging repair job. When the student gets bogged down, he shows a display of temper by banging his tools, cursing, and then sitting and sulking for the remainder of the period. Mr. Potter has had conferences with him about it, and the student keeps insisting that the work is too hard for him. Mr. Potter himself feels that this student has the ability to do the work if he would only develop some patience and perseverance. This show of temper and impatience has apparently had a history of being reinforced long before the student arrived in this class, and Mr. Potter now wants to help establish a more desirable behavior pattern.

75

TURN TO CASE E

What undesirable behavior was winning out over the desirable behavior of working through a solution to the radio repair problems by seeking help and asking questions?

---

cursing, banging tools, sitting and sulking

76

REFER TO CASE E

If Mr. Potter could create a condition to enable the student in his class to be successful, the present undesirable behavior

- ☐ would likely be weakened.
- ☐ would likely continue.

---

would likely be weakened.

77

REFER TO CASE E

Could Mr. Potter identify what was reinforcing the undesirable behavior?

☐ yes ☐ no

---

no

How could Mr. Potter strengthen the behavior of more patience and perseverance?

☐ punish the student for displaying his temper

☐ reinforce him for asking questions, seeking help

---

reinforce him for asking questions, seeking help

78

REFER TO CASE E

What behavior pattern would you try to strengthen, to compete with this student's present display of temper and impatience?

The student should work a problem to completion and/or seek help when he gets bogged down.

79

You have a student who is very shy. She rarely speaks up in class. She rarely talks to other members of the class. Although you can't identify what is maintaining her shy behavior, which of the following determinations on your part might help her to make friends and participate more actively in class?

☐ It's not possible to change a shy person's behavior at all.

☐ I may be able to find some class activity in which this student is successful and pair her with another student whom she may be able to help.

☐ She will respond favorably if I find chances to praise her.

☐ She may participate if she works in a small group on some class project.

I may be able to find some class activity in which this student is successful and pair her with another student whom she may be able to help.

She will respond favorably if I find chances to praise her.

She may participate if she works in a small group on some class project.

80

You have a student who doesn't stick to a task very long and who often daydreams. You decide that he may have emotional problems which you cannot identify.

You conclude:

☐ Since I cannot identify the underlying problems, I cannot attempt to change the behavior.

☐ Although I cannot identify the underlying problems, I might be able to strengthen a more desirable behavior pattern.

Although I cannot identify the underlying problems, I might be able to strengthen a more desirable behavior pattern.

81

When you are unable to identify what is strengthening some undesirable behavior you should proceed by

- ☐ assuming that you cannot change the behavior at all.
- ☐ deciding what will reinforce some competing desirable behavior.
- ☐ punishing the undesirable behavior.

---

deciding what will reinforce some competing desirable behavior.

82

Sometimes you are unable to identify what is strengthening some undesirable behavior. In such a case, how should you proceed?

You should decide what might reinforce (strengthen) the desirable behavior.

83

REVIEW FRAME

In a situation in which you have been **unable to identify** what is reinforcing the undesirable behavior (that is, you are unable to complete step 3), you can, nevertheless, attempt to bring about more desirable behavior.

In such a case you:

decide what will strengthen the desirable behavior.

Now you are ready to begin step 5 in the process of bringing about new behavior: **shaping** the new behavior.

No response required; go on to the next Frame.

84

PREVIEW FRAME

When you have begun to extinguish the old behavior and you have decided on the reinforcer for the new behavior, you are ready to **shape** the new response.*

Behavior is gradually shaped over a period of time. In the frames which follow, you will learn the process of shaping new behavior.

No response required; go on to the next Frame.

CASE F

PART 1

Jack has been asking many questions in class which are not serious; in fact, they are often foolish. He seems to ask them more to get attention than to get information, and he successfully wastes class time by monopolizing the question period.

*If you wish to review the concept of shaping, see the paragraphs on shaping behavior in the chapter called "Principles of Behavior Theory."

Here is an example illustrating the technique for shaping more desirable behavior in Jack.

Day 1: After class, Mr. Forest, the instructor, has a conference with Jack and discusses the difference between serious and foolish questions. He also emphasizes that Jack's interest and participation in class are good, but that questions can serve to help him as well as other class members more if the questions lead to the class's learning something new or interesting, rather than merely giving Jack the opportunity to talk.

Day 2: In class Jack raises his hand and Mr. Forest calls on him. Apparently yesterday's talk did some good because Jack asks a better question than he has in the past. Mr. Forest says, "You've raised a good point, Jack," and answers the question.

Day 3: Jack raises his hand and asks another good question; Mr. Forest says, "I'm glad you've asked about that."

Days 4–5: Jack asks questions that are not as good as the previous days and Mr. Forest answers them but makes no comment about them.

Day 6: Mr. Forest says, "We have time for only one good question." When Jack raises his hand, Mr. Forest does not call him, but on another student.

Day 7: Mr. Forest gives Jack an opportunity to give a report before the class which Jack does with great enthusiasm.

Day 8: During his lecture, Mr. Forest mentions an important idea that Jack raised in class yesterday.

Days 9–11: During the question period, Jack does not raise his hand at all. In an effort to avoid the return of the attention-seeking behavior, Mr. Forest now looks for an opportunity to praise Jack for something he is doing well in class.

Day 12: Jack has been working well in class. He has not been monopolizing the question period, and when he has asked questions, they have been good questions. At the end of Day 12, Mr. Forest says to Jack as he is leaving class, "Jack, I'm very pleased with your effort and class participation!"

CASE F

PART 2

Days 13–20:	Mr. Forest calls on Jack in class, but no more often than he calls on other students.
Day 21:	Mr. Forest praises Jack for bringing up an important idea during a class discussion.
Days 22 on:	Mr. Forest now and then finds occasions for Jack to do extra projects through which he can get attention and receive praise.

85

TURN TO CASE F, PART 1

Case F describes the way an instructor shaped the behavior of one of his students.

Mr. Forest wanted to **weaken** an undesirable behavior and shape a new one.

Match the columns below:

A. Mr. Forest wanted to extinguish (weaken):	1. ______ asking foolish questions
B. Mr. Forest wanted to shape (strengthen):	2. ______ asking serious questions
	3. ______ not asking any questions

---

1. A 2. B 3. neither

86

REFER TO CASE F, PART 1

What was reinforcing Jack's asking foolish questions?

He was getting attention.

87

REFER TO CASE F, Day 5

What did Mr. Forest do to **weaken** Jack's undesirable behavior?

He made no comment (ignored Jack by withholding the reinforcer).

88

REFER TO CASE F, PART 1

On Day 5, Mr. Forest heard Jack's foolish question and made no comment. His aim was to

☐ allow the undesirable behavior to occur and not reinforce it.

☐ prevent the undesirable behavior from occurring by punishing it.

---

allow the undesirable behavior to occur and not reinforce it.

89

REFER TO CASE F, PART 1

Having shown that he could ask better questions, on Day 5 Jack resorted to his old behavior of asking poor ones. By *not* making a comment such as "That was certainly a foolish question, Jack," what method of controlling Jack's behavior was Mr. Forest using?

- ☐ He was not controlling behavior at all.
- ☐ He was punishing Jack.
- ☐ He was reinforcing undesirable behavior.
- ☐ He was using the method of extinction.

He was using the method of extinction.

90

REFER TO CASE F, PART 1

The reinforcer for asking foolish questions in Jack's case was attention. In order to shape more desirable behavior, Mr. Forest

- ☐ provided attention for desirable behavior.
- ☐ withdrew attention altogether.
- ☐ withdrew attention for undesirable behavior.

---

provided attention for desirable behavior.

withdrew attention for undesirable behavior.

91

REFER TO CASE F, PART 1

Praise is often an effective reinforcer in the classroom. On Days 2 and 3, how does Mr. Forest reinforce Jack's asking better questions?

Mr. Forest says: "You've raised a good point. . . . I'm glad you asked that."

92

REFER TO CASE F, PART 1

On Day 6, Jack raises his hand but Mr. Forest does not call on him. He does this to indicate

☐ that Jack will not be called upon if he raises his hand.

☐ that good questions bring attention.

---

that good questions bring attention.

93

REFER TO CASE F, PART 1

On Day 7, Mr. Forest gives Jack the opportunity to make a report. He does this to reinforce

☐ desirable attention-getting behavior.

☐ undesirable attention-getting behavior.

---

desirable attention-getting behavior.

REFER TO CASE F, PART 1

What behavior did Mr. Forest want to change?

Jack's asking foolish questions

What behavior did Mr. Forest want to strengthen instead?

Jack's asking serious questions

How did Mr. Forest weaken the undesirable behavior on Days 4, 5, and 6?

He made no comment about bad questions, and he didn't call on Jack for a few days (both are examples of withdrawing the reinforcer).

How did Mr. Forest positively reinforce the desirable behavior on Days 2 and 3?

He praised Jack by saying, "Good point. . . . I'm glad you asked. . . ."

95

REFER TO CASE F, PART 1

Jack had been getting attention by asking silly questions.

How did Mr. Forest provide opportunities to reinforce Jack's getting attention in a more desirable way?

Your answer should include at least one of the following:

Jack was given the chance to give a report in front of the class.

Jack received praise for raising important points during class discussion.

Jack received praise for his work in class.

96

You want to establish some new behavior. What should you provide to strengthen a desirable new behavior?

You should provide a positive reinforcer.

FOOTNOTE FRAME

Up to this point in the program, you have learned that the most effective way to eliminate an undesirable behavior is to weaken the old behavior by withholding the reinforcer and then to provide a reinforcer to strengthen the new behavior.

Thus far we have not emphasized **punishment** as a means of behavioral control. Since extinction is often a lengthy process, it is not always advisable to wait for a response to extinguish. Instead, the response has sometimes to be suppressed (stopped at once). In such a case, punishment is used. One must, however, be aware that punishment used alone may stop a behavior from occurring, but it will not necessarily help the individual to behave in a more desirable way.

The following case will give you an example of the use of punishment in the process of behavioral change.

No response required; go on to the next Frame.

CASE G

One day in Mr. Greyledge's Auto Body Repair class, Stewart lashed out and hit another student who called him stupid. Stewart was immediately sent out of the room and told to return after school to complete the work he was supposed to have finished in class.

Mr. Greyledge was aware that Stewart was given to venting his anger rather violently and he recognized that he had found only a temporary solution to the problem and had not really changed Stewart's behavior.

98

TURN TO CASE G

Case G is an example of the way an instructor put an immediate stop to the behavior of one of his students.

To what behavior did Mr. Greyledge put a stop?

---

one student's hitting another student

How did Mr. Greyledge handle the problem?

He sent Stewart out of the room and asked him to return after school.

99

REFER TO CASE G

By sending Stewart out of the room, Mr. Greyledge

- ☐ allowed the undesirable behavior to occur without reinforcing it.
- ☐ prevented the undesirable behavior from occurring by suppressing it.

---

prevented the undesirable behavior from occurring by suppressing it.

100

Hitting other students, or other similar violent behavior, cannot be tolerated in a classroom and should be stopped at once. The moment this undesirable behavior occurs, it is

☐ weakened by extinction.

☐ suppressed by punishment.

---

suppressed by punishment.

101

REFER TO CASE G

How did Mr. Greyledge immediately prevent Stewart from continuing to behave in an undesirable way?

He sent Stewart out of the room and made him return after school to make up the work he had missed.

What method did Mr. Greyledge use to begin to stop Stewart from behaving in an undesirable way?

☐ allowing the undesirable behavior to occur and ignoring it to weaken it (extinction)

☐ suppressing the undesirable behavior by using a negative reinforcer (punishment)

---

suppressing the undesirable behavior by using a negative reinforcer (punishment)

102

FOOTNOTE FRAME

The technical distinction between positive reinforcement, negative reinforcement, and punishment is depicted in Exhibit 1. Note that *removing* a *negative* reinforcer is reinforcing (or a reinforcement), just as *giving* a *positive* reinforcer is reinforcement.

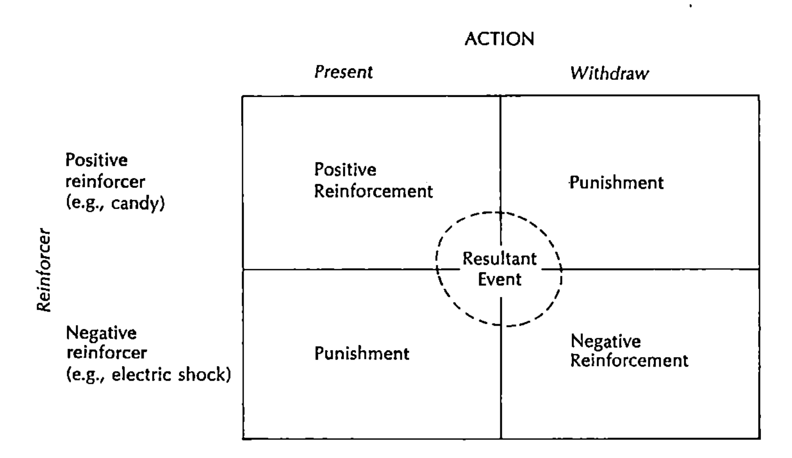

Exhibit 1. Diagrammatic Definition of Reinforcement and Punishment. Note that negative reinforcement increases the behavior that occurred immediately prior to the termination of the noxious stimulus.

No response required; go on to the next Frame.

103

You have just learned two methods of weakening and eliminating undesirable behavior.

In Case F, Part 1, Mr. Forest allowed the undesirable behavior (asking foolish questions) to occur and gradually withdrew attention by ignoring Jack by not calling on him, or by ignoring his questions.

The process of weakening an undesirable response is known as

---

extinction

In Case G, Mr. Greyledge prevented the response of hitting another student from occurring further by sending the student out of the room.

The process of **suppressing** undesirable behavior is known as

---

punishment (negative reinforcer).

104

As part of the process of shaping new behavior, what can you do to **weaken** and **eliminate** the old behavior?

and/or

Your answer should include:

Extinguish it by withholding reinforcement
and/or
suppress it by providing a negative reinforcer (punishment).*

*Punishment should not be overused as a means of controlling behavior.

What can you do to strengthen the new behavior?

Provide a positive reinforcer.

CASE H

Illustrated below is a method some child psychologists suggest to teach a young child how to make his bed.

The psychologists first analyzed the process of bedmaking and saw that it involved the following steps.

1. Pulling the bed away from the wall
2. Pulling back the blankets and top sheet
3. Tightening the bottom sheet
4. Pulling up the top sheet and blankets
5. Tucking in the top sheet and blankets
6. Placing the pillow at the top of the bed
7. Putting the spread on the bed and smoothing it out
8. Tucking the spread under the edge of the pillow
9. Smoothing out the spread
10. Pushing the bed against the wall

Each homemaker probably has her own special procedure for doing this job. The emphasis here is that whatever method is used, there is a series of **steps.** Let's observe a series of lessons in which six-year-old Sandy is taught how to make his bed.

Day 1: "Sandy, watch me make the bed and I'll let you do the last step."

Sandy watches, while Mrs. Holmes makes the bed up to step 10. She then says, "O.K., Sandy, now you push the bed against the wall."

"That's easy."

"Good; tomorrow I'll let you do something harder."

Day 2: Mrs. Holmes makes the bed up to step 7 and then shows Sandy how to tuck the spread under the edge of the pillow. "Sandy, you try it." Sandy pushes the spread too far under the pillow. Mrs. Holmes says, "That's the right idea, Sandy, but the spread should be tucked under the edge, like this." She demonstrates the correct way again. "Now try it once more." Sandy tucks the spread under the pillow unevenly, but better than his first try. Mrs. Holmes says, "That's better, we'll try it again tomorrow. Now, smooth out the spread and push the bed against the wall." Sandy finishes the job. Mrs. Holmes says, "That's fine."

Day 3: Sandy enters saying, "This stuff is easy." Mrs. Holmes says, "I'm glad you think so. Let's try to get the spread to look even smoother today than it looked yesterday." She proceeds to make the bed up to step 7 as Sandy watches. Sandy tucks the spread under the pillow very carefully and smooths out the spread quite well. "Fine, Sandy, I think you're ready to learn another step."

Mrs. Holmes removes the spread from the bed, folds it up, and lays it over a chair in the room. "Sandy, now put the spread on the bed."

Sandy takes the spread and places it on the bed and pulls it up. This step requires some practice as it involves arranging the material so that the spread hangs evenly on all sides. Sandy puts the spread on the bed. "Sandy, what do you do next?"

Sandy proceeds to tuck the spread under the edge of the pillow, smooth out the spread, and push the bed back against the wall.

Day 4: Mrs. Holmes makes the bed up to step 5 and tells Sandy to finish the job. Sandy places the pillow at the top of the bed, places the spread on the bed, and completes the task. Mrs. Holmes says, "You're learning quickly."

Sandy smiles.

Day 5: Mrs. Holmes makes the bed up to step 4 and after she pulls up the top sheet and blankets Sandy immediately begins to tuck them in. This is understandably a hard task for a young child because he does not have the strength to tuck blankets under the mattress so they are smooth and tight. Therefore, some allowance has to be made for his limited ability to do the task well. Some people might decide to eliminate this step and leave the sheet and blankets untucked. Mrs. Holmes says, "I'm glad to see that you knew what to do next, Sandy; that's fine. I'll just help you get some of those hard corners tucked in."

Sandy finishes making the bed through step 10.

Days 6–7: Sandy practices tucking in the top sheet and blanket(s) even tighter and also learns how to pull up the sheet and blanket(s) (step 4).

Day 8: Sandy enters the room and asks, "Mrs. Holmes, may I do the whole thing myself?"

Mrs. Holmes steps aside and watches Sandy make the entire bed. The blanket(s) are a bit wrinkled under the spread and the spread is lopsided, but he has done the whole task in the proper order and with no help. The look on his face when the job is finished is enough to show that he is pleased with himself.

Mrs Homes has noticed only Sandy's success at performing each task. She made no comments about those steps that Sandy did not perform well, and praised Sandy for learning how to do a very complicated job.

105

Shaping new behavior is a step-by-step process and often takes a long time. Old behavior must be extinguished over a period of time, and new behavior must be strengthened.

TURN TO CASE H

Case H describes how a child can be taught to make a bed through the shaping process. The procedure used in this example is easily observed and the process illustrated here may be applied to the process of shaping any new behavior.

Mrs. Holmes recognized that positive reinforcement must follow each correct response in order to strengthen that response.

After Sandy performed each step, Mrs. Holmes gave praise and encouragement.

How did she reinforce Sandy on Days 1 and 2?

On Day 1 Mrs. Holmes said, "Good, now I'll let you do something harder." On Day 2; she said, "That's better. . . . that's fine."

106

REFER TO CASE H

How did Mrs. Holmes make learning bedmaking easier?

Check the statements below which describe how Mrs. Holmes made the task of learning to make a bed easier.

- ☐ She asked Sandy to redo more skillfully the steps which he had demonstrated he could perform.
- ☐ She gave Sandy the opportunity to practice skills he had learned on previous days.
- ☐ She made Sandy redo any steps that he did not do well until he performed it perfectly.
- ☐ She sometimes ignored (by refraining from negative comments) those steps he didn't do entirely correctly.
- ☐ She was often critical when Sandy did not do a particular step well.

She asked Sandy to redo more skillfully the steps which he had demonstrated he could perform.

She gave Sandy the opportunity to practice skills he had learned on previous days.

She sometimes ignored (by refraining from negative comments) those steps he didn't do entirely correctly.

107

On Day 8, Sandy made the whole bed by himself. The job wasn't perfect, but Mrs. Holmes looked for the parts of the task that Sandy performed well and praised him for these.

Mrs. Holmes shaped Sandy's behavior by

- ☐ building on his successes.
- ☐ pointing out his failures.

---

building on his successes.

108

As the student's behavior improves during the shaping process, you can raise the criterion for giving praise.

REFER TO CASE H

If on Day 8 Sandy had **not** tucked in the sheets and placed the spread on the bed as smoothly as he had on Days 5, 6, and 7, Mrs. Holmes would probably have said:

- ☐ "That's fine, Sandy."
- ☐ "You showed me yesterday and the day before that you can do a better job. How about putting the spread on again?"
- ☐ "Sandy, you're not trying."

"You showed me yesterday and the day before that you can do a better job. How about putting the spread on again?"

109

REFER TO CASE H

In shaping the behavior of making a bed, Mrs. Holmes

- ☐ demonstrated the whole task and rewarded only the final behavior of completely making the bed.
- ☐ divided the task into small steps and strengthened one step at a time.

---

divided the task into small steps and strengthened one step at a time.

110

REFER TO CASE H

During the process of shaping, Mrs. Holmes raised the standard for performing each task more correctly

☐ all at once.

☐ gradually.

---

gradually.

111

You have a student with a very short attention span. He cannot sit still in his seat; he rarely completes the projects he starts; he daydreams often. You want to help him attend to each activity for a longer period of time and complete projects he starts.

In order to shape his behavior you should first

☐ allow him to take frequent breaks during the period.

☐ expect him to work at one project for the whole period, as do the other students in the class.

---

allow him to take frequent breaks during the period.

112

During the first stages of shaping a behavior consisting of paying attention, concentrating for longer periods of time, and completing projects, the instructor allows the student to take frequent breaks, and also allows him to work on a variety of activities so that he can vary his focus.

One day the instructor notices that the student has gotten up from his seat less frequently and seems to be working industriously and interestedly at his project. He has not daydreamed at all. Which action(s) below would reinforce this improved behavior?

- ☐ leaving him alone, since he is working so hard
- ☐ walking by his desk and commenting, "I've been noticing how well your project is coming along."
- ☐ saying, "John, since you've been working so hard this period, you may work on that special project you asked me about last week."
- ☐ saying, "John, I always knew you could be a hard worker if you tried."

---

walking by his desk and commenting, "I've been noticing how well your project is coming along."

saying, "John, since you've been working so hard this period, you may work on that special project you asked me about last week."

113

Once you have positively reinforced the student for showing some improvement in his behavior, you can then slowly raise the standards and reinforce him only when he behaves in the improved way. In the case of the student whose span of attention had gradually increased, you will then

- ☐ allow him to take frequent breaks and allow him to work on many different activities in one period.
- ☐ gradually reduce the number of breaks he will be allowed to take and reduce the number of activities on which he will be allowed to work.

---

gradually reduce the number of breaks he will be allowed to take and reduce the number of activities on which he will be allowed to work.

114

You have determined some final behavior which you want to strengthen. During the early stages of the process of shaping you must reinforce

- ☐ any response at all.
- ☐ any response that comes near the desirable behavior.
- ☐ only the final desirable behavior.

---

any response that comes near the desirable behavior.

115

The final desired behavior of the student with the very short attention span is the behavior of working at one task for increasingly longer periods of time, taking fewer breaks, and not daydreaming.

You also expect him to complete his projects before moving on to another activity.

At the end of the shaping process you will, therefore, reinforce

- ☐ handing in completed projects.
- ☐ handing in partially completed projects.
- ☐ taking frequent breaks.
- ☐ taking infrequent breaks.

---

handing in completed projects.
taking infrequent breaks.

116

Check the statements below that are true.

In the process of shaping the behavior of making a bed Mrs. Holmes

- ☐ reinforced one skill at a time in a step-by-step manner.
- ☐ reinforced only perfect or very-near-perfect behavior.
- ☐ suppressed incorrect responses by using punishment.
- ☐ weakened (extinguished) incorrect responses in the early stages of the shaping process by ignoring them.
- ☐ reinforced behavior that came closer to perfection.

---

reinforced one skill at a time in a step-by-step manner.

weakened (extinguished) incorrect responses in the early stages of the shaping process by ignoring them.

reinforced behavior that came closer to perfection.

117

REFER TO CASE H

Describe the shaping process that Mrs. Holmes used to teach Sandy how to make his bed.

She broke the task down into small steps and reinforced each step along the way with praise.

118

The teacher in the classroom situation has the opportunity to build on the successes of his students.

Ralph, a student in your class, has been getting 40% on his tests. On his next test, he gets 60%.

Which of the following would be the best positive reinforcement? Writing:

- ☐ "60% = failing."
- ☐ "This is an improvement over your last test. Keep it up!"
- ☐ "Try to do better next time."
- ☐ nothing—because the student is still failing and you do not want to discourage him by saying anything at this time.

"This is an improvement over your last test. Keep it up!"

119

A student has been asking foolish questions. In order to strengthen his asking good questions you would first help him recognize the difference between a good question and a foolish question.

You would then shape his behavior by providing positive reinforcement for behavior that comes closer and closer to the final desirable behavior.

Put the following steps in order:

_______ Praise the student each time he asks a serious question.

_______ Praise the student now and then for asking a good question.

_______ Ignore all foolish questions.

2, 3, 1

120

When shaping any new behavior, the instructor must provide

---

positive reinforcer(s).

How does the instructor help the student arrive at the final behavior (that is, how does the instructor **shape** the final behavior)?

The instructor reinforces behavior that comes closer and closer to the final behavior.

121

Place the following steps in the correct sequence:

_______ **Identify** the reinforcer of the undesirable behavior.

_______ **Identify** the undesirable behavior that exists. **Identify** the desirable behavior that should be strengthened and **discuss** the student's behavior with him.

_______ **Obtain** suggestions from the student as to ways he can change his own behavior; **give** your own suggestions; **explain** your objections to his behavior.

_______ **Shape** the new behavior by reinforcing behavior that comes closer to the final behavior.

_______ **Withhold** the reinforcer for the undesirable behavior and **decide** what will reinforce the new behavior.

3, 1, 2, 5, 4

122

You have identified an undesirable behavior and a desirable behavior that you would like to strengthen instead (step 1).

You have obtained suggestions and/or made suggestions of your own as to ways to bring about the new behavior (step 2).

You have identified what the student is getting out of behaving in an undesirable way (step 3).

You have begun to weaken the old behavior by withholding the reinforcer, and you have decided what reinforcer will strengthen the new behavior (step 4).

What is your next step?

---

to shape the new behavior

123

REVIEW FRAME

You have now completed the **fifth** step in the process of behavior change.

You have:

shaped desired behavior

by

positively reinforcing behavior that comes closer and closer to some final behavior

and by

building one skill upon another in a step-by-step manner.

You are now ready to begin step 6: **maintaining** the new behavior.

No response required; go on to the next Frame.

124

PREVIEW FRAME

You have thus far learned how to carry out part of the behavior change process. You have learned how to extinguish (weaken and eliminate) an undesirable behavior and how to shape (strengthen) a new behavior in its place.

Once a desirable behavior has been shaped, the student will continue to respond in this new way if his newly acquired behavior is followed by positive reinforcement. You will now learn how to **maintain** newly acquired behavior.

No response required; go on to the next Frame.

125

REFER BACK TO CASE F, PART 1

In shaping Jack's behavior, Mr. Forest reinforced Jack by praising every good question he asked. He also gave Jack frequent opportunities to get attention in desirable ways by calling on him often in class and by providing him with extra projects to do.

When Mr. Forest was first shaping Jack's behavior, he reinforced Jack's desirable attention-getting behavior of asking good questions and doing well in class

☐ nearly every time Jack responded in a desirable way.

☐ only now and then.

---

nearly every time Jack responded in a desirable way.

126

REFER BACK TO CASE F, PART 2

The conclusion of this case describes how Mr. Forest maintained Jack's newly acquired behavior.

On Days 13–20, did Mr. Forest give Jack as many opportunities to receive reinforcement for his new behavior as he had before?

☐ yes

☐ no

---

no

127

REFER BACK TO CASE F, PART 1

When a new response is first shaped, the student receives a reinforcement, such as praise,

☐ for nearly every correct response.

☐ only occasionally.

---

for nearly every correct response.

128

REFER BACK TO CASE F, PART 2

On Days 13–21, Mr. Forest

☐ shaped new behavior by reinforcing nearly every correct re-response.

☐ maintained new behavior by reinforcing Jack only occasionally.

---

maintained new behavior by reinforcing Jack only occasionally.

When you are shaping new behavior, you reinforce almost every correct response. This is called a *continuous reinforcement schedule.**

When you want to maintain behavior that has already been shaped, you reinforce this behavior from time to time. This is called an *occasional reinforcement schedule.**

If you wished to give Neil **continuous** reinforcement to shape his behavior of handing in complete, rather than partially complete, projects, you would

☐ occasionally make a favorable comment to Neil about his effort to complete his projects.

☐ praise Neil each time he hands in a completed project.

☐ praise Neil only at times when his projects are complete and done perfectly.

☐ rarely praise Neil, because no student deserves praise for merely completing a project.

---

praise Neil each time he hands in a completed project.

If you feel that Neil's behavior is now adequately strengthened and you want to give him occasional reinforcement, you should

☐ discontinue making any comments when he completes a project.

☐ every time that Neil completes a project say, "I'm glad to see you finally completed your project."

☐ now and then say, "Neil, your projects are showing much more effort."

*The word *schedule* as it used here means the frequency with which reinforcements are provided when shaping or maintaining behavior.

now and then say, "Neil, your projects are showing much more effort."

130

You have a student, Tim, who used to interrupt you by calling out questions and answers before he was called upon. You have shaped Tim's behavior well, so that when he wants to enter into a class discussion he no longer shouts out from his seat and almost always raises his hand. If you want to maintain this behavior, you should

- ☐ call on Tim every time he raises his hand.
- ☐ call on Tim no more often than you call on other students, and every now and then say, "Tim, you raised a good question. I'm glad you waited until I finished my point before you asked it."
- ☐ every time he raises his hand say, "Tim, I'm glad to see that you raised your hand."

---

call on Tim no more often than you call on other students, and every now and then say, "Tim, you raised a good question. I'm glad you waited until I finished my point before you asked it."

131

REFER BACK TO CASE F, PART 2

How did Mr. Forest maintain Jack's behavior of asking serious questions and of getting attention in desirable ways?

---

by finding occasions to praise Jack now and then

132

You would use a **continuous** reinforcement schedule in the behavior change process when you are

- ☐ maintaining a new behavior.
- ☐ shaping a new behavior.
- ☐ suppressing behavior.

---

shaping a new behavior.

You would use an **occasional** reinforcement schedule in the behavior change process when you are

- ☐ extinguishing an undesirable behavior.
- ☐ maintaining a new behavior.
- ☐ shaping a new behavior.
- ☐ suppressing behavior.

---

maintaining a new behavior.

133

When you first start shaping a new behavior, what reinforcement schedule is most effective?

---

a continuous reinforcement schedule

After the new behavior is sufficiently strengthened, what reinforcement schedule is most effective?

---

an occasional reinforcement schedule

134

REVIEW FRAME

You have now completed the **sixth** step in the process of behavior change.

You have

maintained the desired behavior
by
reinforcing the desired behavior occasionally

You are now ready to begin step 7, the final step in the behavior change process.

No response required; go on to the next Frame.

135

PREVIEW FRAME

You have now worked through the whole process of behavioral change, from **identifying** and then **extinguishing** some undesirable behavior, to **shaping** and **maintaining** some new desirable behavior in its place. If you occasionally reinforce the desirable behavior with praise, encouragement, attention, or whatever else may be the appropriate reinforcer, this behavior is very likely to continue. However, there may be instances when the old behavior reoccurs. This may happen for one or more of several reasons: the old behavior may not really have been extinguished; the new behavior may not yet have been strengthened sufficiently; the original identification of the problem, and the behavioral objectives set for the student, may not have been appropriately defined; or, generally, one's past actions may not have been adequate to solve the problem.

In the following frames you will learn what to do if the old behavior recurs.

No response required; go on to the next Frame.

136

You have a student who has been standing around idly and not participating in class activities. You tried to provide opportunities for this student to be successful so that he would receive praise. The student then began to participate actively and he was doing very well. However, each time you start a new project, this student resorts to his old pattern of standing around idly and watching the other students.

Which of the following would you do to **reshape** his behavior?

☐ Ignore him, expecting that if he is left alone he'll begin to participate again on his own.

☐ Say, "John, if you will not work, please leave the room."

☐ Say, "John, you can do it. Why don't you begin and I'll help you if you run into a problem."

Say, "John, you can do it. Why don't you begin and I'll help you if you run into a problem."

CASE I

Tracy, a girl in Mrs. Shaw's Commercial English class, habitually sought approval of every step of her work before she had completed even one section of the assignment. She repeatedly came to Mrs. Shaw asking her to read over what she had written or to check her spelling or to give her ideas. Mrs. Shaw spent several months shaping Tracy's behavior so that she would bring up her papers only when she had completed whole sections, and would seek help only when she could not proceed further on a problem without help. Tracy reached the stage where she was able to work independently for several consecutive days without assistance from Mrs. Shaw.

However, Mrs. Shaw subsequently noticed that when a new subject or project was introduced in class, Tracy reverted to her old pattern of coming up many times during the period to ask if her work were satisfactory or to receive some kind of special assistance. Mrs. Shaw concluded that a possible approach would be to continue the original shaping process to bring about greater independence in Tracy, since the new behavior had apparently not been as firmly established as Mrs. Shaw had thought. In considering Tracy's behavior she concluded that her own efforts to help Tracy work more independently in the past had not provided Tracy with the kind of help she needed to maintain her new independent work habits.

Mrs. Shaw felt that Tracy might respond to more structure than she had been provided with in the past and decided to take the following action: The next time Tracy came up for advice or help on her papers Mrs. Shaw planned to write out a list of concrete suggestions describing exactly what Tracy should do to improve, on the assumption that merely telling Tracy orally might not provide enough help. The ultimate aim would be to enable the skill of criticizing her own papers. As a starter, Mrs. Shaw would help Tracy develop a checklist of things to look for in her writing which Tracy would be able to use to evaluate her own work. She also felt that it would be necessary to establish with Tracy a maximum number of times that she could come up to have her incomplete papers appraised. Gradually this number would be reduced so that Tracy would seek this kind of attention less and less. While this reshaping process was under way, Mrs. Shaw planned to continue looking for opportunities to praise Tracy on her work. On those days that Tracy was able to work by herself with only minimal extra attention, Mrs. Shaw would be sure to let Tracy know how well she had independently followed through on the assignment.

137

TURN TO CASE I

Read paragraphs 1 and 2.

What behavior had Mrs. Shaw tried to shape originally?

---

working independently; completing projects without undue extra assistance

Had this behavior been adequately strengthened?

☐ yes

☐ no

---

no

138

REFER TO CASE I

Mrs. Shaw reevaluated her past actions in shaping Tracy's behavior and concluded that Tracy

☐ could not be expected to work independently.

☐ was capable of displaying greater independence.

---

was capable of displaying greater independence.

139

REFER TO CASE I

Mrs. Shaw decided that the original objectives she had set for Tracy weren't wrong, but that the new behavior (independent work habits; not seeking extra attention) had not been sufficiently strengthened.

What did Mrs. Shaw do **first** to help Tracy regain independence?

She began reshaping Tracy's behavior by providing her with a checklist to help her to evaluate her own papers.

140

REFER TO CASE I

Having been provided with a self-evaluation checklist, Tracy would probably be

☐ as likely to seek attention from Mrs. Shaw as before.

☐ less likely to seek attention from Mrs. Shaw than before.

☐ more likely to seek attention from Mrs. Shaw than before.

---

less likely to seek attention from Mrs. Shaw than before.

141

REFER TO CASE I

As part of the process of **reshaping** Tracy's behavior, Mrs. Shaw would gradually provide Tracy with

☐ less assistance.

☐ more assistance.

---

less assistance.

142

REFER TO CASE I

In the final stages of the reshaping process, Mrs. Shaw would give praise and encouragement only when

☐ Tracy demanded a little less attention than formerly.

☐ Tracy displayed almost complete independence.

Tracy displayed almost complete independence.

143

REFER TO CASE I

What behavior of Tracy's did Mrs. Shaw want to reshape?

---

her ability to work independently

What did Mrs. Shaw do to reshape Tracy's behavior?

Your answer should include at least one of the following:

She provided more structure by offering suggestions to help Tracy improve and by working out a self-evaluation list.

She found occasions to praise Tracy.

She told Tracy that she was capable of doing the work.

144

REFER TO CASE I

When Tracy's old behavior recurred, Mrs. Shaw decided that the new behavior had not been adequately strengthened.

What action did she take?

☐ She gave up.

☐ She ignored the problem.

☐ She punished the student.

☐ She reshaped the behavior.

She reshaped the behavior.

145

In some cases when an undesirable behavior reoccurs, the reoccurrence is attributable to inappropriate past actions taken in attempts to solve the problem.

For example, suppose you have a student who had frequently been absent from your class. You had a conference with him and discovered that he thought the work was too hard and he couldn't do most of the assignments. You gave him a great deal of individual help, both in and out of class. He began to come to class more regularly and participated more actively than he had in the past. You had hoped to help him develop skills and study habits that would aid him in solving problems in your course and would thereby contribute toward improving his attitude toward school, but recently he has begun complaining of headaches or stomach aches immediately before the start of your class. You have investigated the matter and learned that there is actually nothing wrong with the student's health.

You have decided that perhaps you expected too much from the student. In reevaluating the problem, which of the following would be appropriate judgments for you to consider?

- ☐ The student can't handle your class and, therefore, you should have him transferred from it.
- ☐ The student doesn't like you and, therefore, should have a different instructor.
- ☐ The student may have additional problems which you cannot identify, and you should refer the problem to professional services, such as guidance or psychological counselors.
- ☐ There may be too few or no opportunities for positive reinforcement in your class.
- ☐ You may not have provided the student with the right kind of help, and the work may still really be too difficult for him.

The student may have additional problems which you cannot identify, and you should refer the problem.

There may be too few or no opportunities for positive reinforcement in your class.

You may not have provided the student with the right kind of help, and the work may still really be too difficult for him.

146

REFER TO CASE I

Read Paragraph 3.

Not only did Mrs. Shaw decide to reshape Tracy's behavior, she

- ☐ concluded that she had done all the right things in the first place and that Tracy was too difficult to change.
- ☐ decided to use the same procedures that she had the first time when shaping Tracy's behavior.
- ☐ reexamined her own past actions in changing Tracy's behavior, and concluded that she had not come up with the best solutions.

---

reexamined her own past actions in changing Tracy's behavior, and concluded that she had not come up with the best solutions.

147

Although you have shaped a new behavior, the old behavior might recur. If you decide to reshape the new behavior, you should also reexamine the actions you originally took in bringing about the new behavior.

REFER TO CASE A: Conclusions 1 and 2

If Claudia reverts to being uncooperative when working with her group, and Mrs. Grant wants to reshape her behavior, she would probably

☐ assess whether or not Claudia is getting the necessary attention and praise to strengthen cooperative behavior.

☐ decide that Claudia is stubborn and simply wait for her to cooperate.

☐ evaluate the solutions that had been suggested by herself and by the group to help Claudia participate in a more cooperative manner.

☐ remove Claudia from all group activities.

---

assess whether or not Claudia is getting the necessary attention and praise to strengthen cooperative behavior.

evaluate the solutions that had been suggested by herself and by the group to help Claudia participate in a more cooperative manner.

148

In the event that the undesirable behavior begins to recur, you take two final actions in the process of behavior change:

You **reshape**

and

you **reexamine**

---

the new behavior

your own past actions

149

You have shaped a new behavior pattern in a student (step 6).
One day the old undesirable behavior begins to recur in class.

What actions should you take now (step 7)?

and/or

You should **reshape** the new behavior
and/or
reexamine your past actions in the behavior change process.

150

REVIEW FRAME

Now you have brought about a new behavior in a student. In the event that the undesirable behavior recurs, you must:

reshape the new behavior

and

reexamine your past actions in the behavior change process

This is the final step (step 7) in the process of bringing about desirable behavior in your students.

No response required; go on to the next Frame.

151

REVIEW FRAME

Let's review the whole process of behavior change, using the example of Claudia in Case A.

What behavior did Mrs. Grant want to change?

REFER TO CASE A (if necessary)

Claudia's uncooperative group behavior

How would you describe the first action Mrs. Grant took in the process of changing Claudia's behavior?

She identified the undesirable behavior.

152

REFER TO CASE A (if necessary)

After Mrs. Grant had identified that Claudia was uncooperative and bossy, what else did she identify as part of the first step in the process of bringing about new behavior?

She identified the behavior that should occur instead.

153

Mrs. Grant determined that Claudia should learn to listen to the ideas of others and offer her own ideas as suggestions, rather than impose them as final decisions.

What further action did Mrs. Grant take in the first step of the behavior change process in order to make Claudia aware of her own problem behavior?

Mrs. Grant held a conference with Claudia to discuss Claudia's uncooperative group behavior.

154

REVIEW FRAME FOR STEP 1

What actions do you take in the first step of the behavior change process?

> **Identify:**
> **Identify:**
> **Discuss:**

---

the undesirable behavior

the desirable behavior that should occur instead

the student's behavior with him

Note: If you had any difficulty with Frames 151–154, you may wish to review step 1 in the program—Frames 1–18.

155

REFER TO CASES A AND B (if necessary)

During the conference with Claudia (Case A), Mrs. Grant learned that her student **did not** recognize her own "problem" behavior; while in Case B, Mrs. Sanford learned that Joel **did** recognize his "problem" behavior.

How did the instructors in each case arrive at suggestions for changing the undesirable behavior in their respective students?

Match the columns below:

A. The instructor offered suggestions.

B. The instructor obtained suggestions from the student.

1. ______ Mrs. Grant

2. ______ Mr. Sanford

---

1. A. 2. A and B

REFER TO CASE A (if necessary)

If the student can't offer suggestions as to how to change his behavior, what should the instructor do?

He should offer his own suggestions.

157

REFER TO CASE A (if necessary)

During the teacher-student conference, how can the instructor get the student to participate in bringing about a change in his own behavior?

He can ask the student to offer suggestions.

158

If the student has no suggestions to offer, the group isn't very helpful, and the instructor has difficulty interpreting the old behavior and making suggestions to help bring about the new behavior, what other sources are available to the instructor for further suggestions?

---

guidance and psychological services

159

REVIEW FRAME FOR STEP 2

What actions do you take in the second step of the behavior change process?

Obtain suggestions from:

Offer suggestions from:

Consult:

---

the student himself, and/or the class

yourself

guidance, psychological, or, other resource people

Note: If you had difficulty with Frames 155–159, you may wish to review step 2 in the program—Frames 19–36.

160

REFER TO CASE A (if necessary)

Mrs. Grant believed that Claudia's overbearing and domineering group behavior was one way for her to get attention and recognition.

Mrs. Grant was **identifying:**

- ☐ a method for changing Claudia's behavior.
- ☐ the undesirable behavior.
- ☐ what Claudia was getting out of being uncooperative (the reinforcer for the undesirable behavior).

---

what Claudia was getting out of being uncooperative (the reinforcer for the undesirable behavior).

161

REVIEW FRAME FOR STEP 3

You have identified the undesirable behavior and the desirable behavior and you have discussed the student's behavior with him (step 1). You have also obtained suggestions from the student, obtained any needed information from outside resource people, and made suggestions of your own (step 2). What do you identify in **step 3** before you can take any further action?

You identify what is reinforcing the undesirable behavior.

Note: If you had difficulty with Frames 160 and 161, you may wish to review step 3 in the program—Frames 37–53.

162

Once the reinforcers for the undesirable behavior have been identified, the old behavior is weakened or extinguished by

withholding

---

the reinforcer for the undesirable behavior.

New behavior is strengthened by

deciding upon

---

the reinforcer for the desirable behavior.

163

REFER TO CASE A (if necessary)

Once the reinforcers for Claudia's behavior had been identified, how could the undesirable behavior be extinguished (weakened)?

---

by withholding the reinforcer

Even if the reinforcers for Claudia's behavior had not been identified, what could the instructor decide upon in order to bring about more desirable behavior?

He could decide upon the reinforcer(s) for more cooperative behavior.

164

REVIEW FRAME FOR STEP 4

What action do you take to weaken or extinguish undesirable behavior?

---

withhold the reinforcer for the undesirable behavior

What action do you take before you can strengthen desirable behavior?

---

decide upon the reinforcer for the desirable behavior.

Note: If you had difficulty with Frames 162–164, you may wish to review step 4 in the program—Frames 54–72 and 73–83.

165

After you have decided upon the reinforcer to strengthen the new behavior, you **shape** the new behavior.

Describe the shaping process.

You reinforce behavior which comes closer and closer to some final behavior in a step-by-step manner.

166

REVIEW FRAME FOR STEP 5

Now you have started to extinguish the old, undesirable behavior and you have decided upon the reinforcer to strengthen the new desirable behavior (step 4). You are ready to bring about a new behavior.

You use the process known as:

---

shaping.

Note: If you had any difficulty with these frames, you may wish to review step 5 in the program—Frames 84–123.

167

Once Claudia's cooperative group behavior is shaped (that is, she allows other group members to actively participate in the planning sessions, listening to the ideas of others and sharing her own ideas without imposing her opinions on the group), and this desirable behavior is established through the use of continuous reinforcement, what reinforcement schedule is necessary to **maintain** the new behavior?

---

occasional reinforcement schedule

168

REVIEW FRAME FOR STEP 6

After the desirable behavior is shaped, what is the next step for making certain that the desirable behavior continues?

Maintain the behavior, using occasional reinforcement.

Note: If you had any difficulty with Frames 167 and 168, you may wish to review step 6 in the program—Frames 124–134.

169

REVIEW FRAME FOR STEP 7

REFER TO CASE A (if necessary)

Through the shaping process, Claudia has become a cooperative group member. What if she suddenly slipped back into being bossy and uncooperative?

What actions would you take?

and/or

Reshape her behavior
and/or
reexamine your past actions in the behavior change process.

Note: If you had any difficulty with this frame, you may wish to review step 7 in the program—Frames 135–150.

Place the following in the proper sequence:

_______ Identify the behavior that you wish to eliminate and identify the new behavior that you wish to strengthen; hold a conference with the student.

_______ Identify the possible reinforcers for the undesirable behavior and determine who or what is providing the reinforcement for the undesirable behavior.

_______ Maintain the new behavior by using positive reinforcement, moving from a continuous reinforcement schedule to an occasional reinforcement schedule.

_______ Obtain suggestions from the student about ways to change his behavior; explain your own objections to his behavior; offer your own suggestions; consult with guidance services.

_______ Reshape the new behavior (if the old behavior recurs) and/or reexamine your past actions in the behavior change process.

_______ Select a reinforcer that you think will strengthen the new behavior, and withhold the reinforcer for the undesirable behavior (extinction) or suppress the old behavior.

_______ Shape the new behavior.

1, 3, 6, 2, 7, 4, 5

END OF PROGRAM. YOU ARE NOW READY TO TAKE THE POST-TESTS on page 197.

REVIEWING THE BEHAVIOR CHANGE PROCESS

	Teaching Frames	*Review Frames*
STEP 1 **Identify** the behavior that you wish to eliminate and **identify** the new behavior that you wish to strengthen; hold a conference with the student.	1–18	151–154
STEP 2 **Obtain** suggestions from the student about ways to change his behavior; **explain** your own objections to his behavior; **offer** your own suggestions; **consult** with guidance services.	19–36	155–159
STEP 3 **Identify** the possible reinforcers for the undesirable behavior and determine who or what is providing the reinforcement for the undesirable behavior.	37–53	160–161
STEP 4 Decide upon a reinforcer that you think will strengthen the new behavior, and **withhold** the reinforcer for the undesirable behavior (extinction) or suppress the old behavior.	54–72 and 73–83	162–164
STEP 5 **Shape** the new behavior.	84–123	165–166
STEP 6 **Maintain** the new behavior by using positive reinforcement, moving from a continuous reinforcement schedule to an occasional reinforcement schedule.	124–134	167–168
STEP 7 **Reshape** the new behavior (if the old behavior recurs) and/or **reexamine** your past actions in the behavior change process.	135–150	169

RESEARCH NOTES

ments. Generalizability and external validity rest on the ability to demonstrate the principle across individual subjects (*Ss*) or students. Thus, although it has at times been misinterpreted, the research strategy does not propose to extrapolate its findings from a single organism to a given population.

Another way in which this general paradigm differs from more conventional experimental "group" designs is its emphasis upon observing the individual's behavior over a relatively longer period of time. While the traditional group laboratory experiment, particularly for human subjects, rarely involves more than a few hours, behavior change studies often extend over weeks and even years. An experimental history of long duration allows the nontransitory effects of "learning-to-learn" (Harlow, 1949) and other longitudinal concomittants to operate and be observed.

The fundamental premise is that if a reinforcement (reinforcing stimulus) immediately follows a response, the probability that the response will be emitted again on a subsequent occasion is increased. Thus, if the elimination of undesirable behavior is the object, then the reinforcing stimulus that is maintaining the undesirable response should be identified and withdrawn. Further, a stimulus that will strengthen and maintain desired behavior may be identified and consistently administered following performance of, or gradual approximations of, the desired response. Tasks during this shaping process are set at levels that allow the subject to experience frequent success. By gradually increasing the criterion of correct performance, *E* leads *S* to the desired response. The reinforcing stimulus may be in the form of a reward (positive reinforcement) or in the form of termination of a noxious stimulus (negative reinforcement). One response may even serve as a reinforcing stimulus for another behavior: That is, if behavior B (with neutral scholastic value) has a higher probability of occurrence than behavior A (which has positive scholastic value), then the frequency of behavior A can be increased by using the privilege of doing B as a reinforcer for behavior A (Premack, 1959).

The allegation that such a paradigm "bribes people to do what they should do on their own" is totally lacking in validity. Children *learn* to behave in ways that the significant others in their lives consider correct, and the learning is accomplished as a consequence of many material and social response-contingent reinforcements. Unfortunately, some individuals, because of the physical or social effects of disadvantagement or other circumstances, have not been provided adequate opportunity to learn or maintain certain behaviors. The teacher who objects strongly to rewarding a student for desired behavior would, in all likelihood, not work himself if his reinforcements (money, social approval, accomplishment) were terminated (Meyerson, Kerr, and Michael, 1967).

INDIVIDUAL APPLICATION

In the few years that researchers and educators have attempted practical application of knowledge gained through basic instrumental conditioning research, projects have ranged from instigation of the learning of a simple motor response to instituting total "token economies" for the individuals of an entire ward or classroom. Concrete or tangible reinforcement has been particularly effective for promoting learning by seriously disadvantaged individuals. Using a warm sugar-milk solution as a reinforcing stimulus, Fuller (1949) was able, in a short period of time, to bring about the learning of a purposive arm movement in an 18-year-old "vegetative" human who had previously demonstrated no learning.

Crosson and de Jung (1967) were able to train individual severely retarded males (mean I.Q. 27) to function effectively in prescribed vocational settings by utilizing candy combined with verbal and other forms of social reinforcement. For example, machine operation for the manufacture of wooden pencil holders was mastered within three hours, and retention following a two-month interval approached 100 per cent.

Rewarding an autistic child with ice cream promoted glasses-wearing behavior (Wolf, Risley, and Mees, 1964). Relatively complex repertories of discrimination were developed by autistic children in order to gain coins that could be redeemed for entertainment involving a pinball machine, a trained monkey, an electric train, a television, trinkets, or various candies (Ferster and DeMyer, 1962). In that investigation, coins acquired sufficient secondary reinforcing properties to promote saving and an acceptance of a delay of primary reinforcement, behaviors which are generally considered incompatible with autism. Withdrawal of music was involved in suppressing and extinguishing the self-destructive behavior of one schizophrenic child (Lovass, Freitag, Gold, and Kassorla, 1965).

M & M candies, together with praise for appropriate and productive classroom behavior, reduced the rate of vomiting and tantruming to zero in thirty days for a mentally retarded girl. This child, who was diagnosed as suffering from cerebral palsy, aphasia, hyperirritability, and brain damage, had vomitted as many as 21 times in a single day (Wolf, Birnbrauer, Williams, and Lawler, 1965). A combination of M & Ms and social reinforcers proved successful in the implementation of a learning theory approach to the treatment of a school-phobic child (Patterson, 1965). It was demonstrated (Baer, 1962) that thumbsucking behavior of a 5-year-old could be controlled by interrupting the picture and sound track of cartoons the child was watching.

Some further applications of behavior modification techniques to physical, sensory, and emotional rehabilitation have yielded promising data. In the case of a child with cerebral palsy, for example, tokens (tradable for other items) that were dispensed contingent upon gradual approximations of falling correctly and safely on command overcame fear of falling. Before the introduction of this procedure, Meyerson, Kerr, and Michael (1967) report that the boy could not be induced to stand alone. These authors also report the success of similar procedures in encouraging a 9-year-old mentally retarded child to walk for the first time, and in virtually eliminating, through provision of tactually stimulating conditions, the self-destructive behavior of an autistic child. A traumatic quadriplegic adolescent's motivation to learn to type was markedly influenced by altering the discriminative stimulus associated with the task (a different room) and modifying the pattern of the occupational therapist's attention-giving responses (Meyerson, *et al.*, 1967). In another case, a novel device called a "posture switch" (Azrin, Rubin, O'Brien, Ayllon, and Roll, 1968) was attached to a subject's neck and shoulders and was concealed from view by outer garments. This portable operant treatment instrument, which provided an aversive warning tone for the duration of slouching, was effective in promoting postural change.

Staats indicates that encouraging results have been obtained in the development of more difficult prosthetic responses when they are followed by the receipt of tokens that have acquired secondary reinforcing properties for the physically disadvantaged child. Before developing skill with a prosthesis, a child may gain reinforcement more easily for substitution movements that are already within his repertoire. Thus, it would be highly desirable, at first, to provide extrinsic reinforcing stimuli for the more difficult responses, ". . . since, in a competitive sense, these responses are not themselves 'naturally' reinforcing" (Staats, 1964, p. 138).

Adults as well as children have benefitted from such behavioristic-systems approaches. Ayllon (1965) reports that one schizophrenic's failure to go voluntarily to the dining room and eat unaided, a behavior that had persisted for 16 years, and another's failure to leave the dining room unaided were readily corrected by a simple combination of food and social reinforcers. In another application Ayllon (1963) describes the control of food stealing by food withdrawal, control of towel hoarding by providing excessive towels, and control of excessive clothing wear through food reinforcement. A number of practical techniques that apply to the problem of uncontrolled eating and in the treatment of obesity have been discussed by Ferster, Nurnberger, and Levitt (1962).

As with the case of the schizophrenic child cited earlier, music that the patient had selected to hear from the hospital music library was an effective reinforcer in a study by Barrett (1962). In that investigation, reduction in the rate of multiple tics emitted by a 38-year-old veteran was achieved by tic-contingent interruption of the selected music.

Additionally, operant techniques have been instrumental in the experimental analysis and treatment of hysterical blindness (Brady and Lind, 1961), nervous anorexia (Lang, 1965), a fetish which had persisted for 21 years (Kushner, 1965), snake phobia (Lang and Lazovik, 1963), and various other phobic disorders (Lazarus, 1961). Further illustrations of the power of reinforcement therapy include such diverse examples as the treatment of a sexually inadequate man (Lazarus, 1965), exhibitionism (Bond and Hutchison, 1960), and complete toilet training of a 19-month-old child in 12 days (Madsen, 1965).

Verbal behavior has proven particularly amenable to the influence of appropriate reinforcement (Hart and Risley, 1968; Risley and Wolf, 1966; Wolf, Risley, and Mees, 1964; Rheingold, Gewirtz, and Ross, 1959). For autistic children, mimicking has been encouraged to reach desired ends through appetitive reinforcing stimuli, and undesirable echolalia has been extinguished. Lip movement and subsequent meaningful vocalizations were reinstated in two chronic withdrawn psychotics who had been mute for 19 and 14 years respectively, through the use of chewing gum as a reinforcing stimulus (Isaacs, Thomas, and Goldiamond, 1960). Stuttering has been the object of control for several authors employing this paradigm (Flanagan, Goldiamond, and Azrin, 1958; Rickard and Mundy, 1965; Goldiamond, 1965). Social reinforcement, together with such response-contingent consequences as blasts of aversive noise and electric shock, have been found effective in reducing the incidence of stuttering.

Verbal conditioning studies have demonstrated that the content of casual conversation can be influenced by social or supportive reinforcement (Verplanck, 1955). However, there is controversy as to the influence of a subject's degree of awareness of the response-reinforcement contingency (Dulany, 1962). Saslow (1965) states that the length of time a person talks about whatever topic he happens to be on at a given time can be increased by 50 percent merely by the listener's nodding his head intermittently. Saslow describes the case of a man who would talk about nothing except his minor physical ailments. The man began to recall and speak of other facets of his life when he no longer was accorded sympathetic listeners. He began to work for the first time in 15 years following his understanding that social reinforcement would be contingent upon non-complaint verbalization.

Although the major proportion of studies cited to this point have utilized tangible reinforcers in conjunction with intangible social ones, the power of the latter, alone, is well documented (Hall, Lund, and Jackson, 1968; Rickard and Dinoff, 1962; Harris, Wolf, and Baer, 1964; Allen, Hart, Buell, Harris, and Wolf, 1964; Williams, 1959). For instance, through these methods one child left behind his inappropriate crawling behavior and learned to be on his feet, while another—an excessively passive and timid boy—learned to approach and play on climbing frame equipment. These are examples where the giving of attention reinforced the desired instrumental behavior of children, just as it had done in the study of the complaining adult.

Additionally, reports of extinction of undesirable behaviors when attention was withheld are numerous. For example, extinction of the crying and tantrum episodes of normal, retarded, and emotionally disturbed children has been achieved through withdrawal of adult social reinforcement, in the form of attention giving after putting the child to bed or whatever occasion, contingent on the occurrence of the problem behavior.

COOPERATION AND GROUP APPLICATION

There have been a number of attempts to apply behavior change principles to group situations. Although dissemination of the results of such attempts has thus far been confined largely to mimeographed progress reports, several reports have appeared. In one widely cited study by Azrin and Lindsley (1956) jelly beans and a red light were sufficient to develop and maintain as well as to eliminate cooperation between children. Hingtgen, Sanders, and DeMyer (1965) investigated the cooperative behavior of early childhood schizophrenics. Coins that could be exchanged for candy, crackers, or dry cereal strengthened the desired cooperative lever-pressing responses for these children who were incapable of recognizing the superordinate nature of the tasks. In a later paper, Hingtgen (Hingtgen and Trost, 1966) describes a similar situation in which mutual physical contact and vocal responses were shaped. Among highly withdrawn schizophrenic adults, candy, pictures, and cigarettes were used as reinforcing stimuli to shape initial instrumental responses and subsequent cooperation (King, Armitage, and Filton, 1960).

Learning therapy and behavior modification principles are not particularly difficult to apply in many cases. Undergraduates (Davison, 1965), teachers, nurses, aides, parents, and children have appropriately dispensed social as well as tangible reinforcing stimuli. For example, mothers acting as behavior therapists successfully reduced excessive aggressive, dependent, and/or stubborn behaviors in their own children (Zeilberger, Sampen, and Sloane, 1968; Wahler, Winkle, Peterson, and Morrison, 1965).

Although individual plans of remediation were specified for 19 patients in a mental hospital, Ayllon and Michael (1959) report that the nursing staff was able, cooperatively, to carry on effective combinations of extinction, reinforcement, and avoidance programs. Ayllon and Haughton (1962) found that a group of 45 chronic schizophrenics were soon eating unassisted when they learned that refusal to eat was no longer followed by social reinforcement. In addition, all these patients learned motor and social responses to gain access to the dining area. A group of 26 assaultive, retarded females with I.Q. 5 to 25 learned acceptable dining room behavior when satiation was dependent upon such behavior (Edwards and Lily, 1966). These authors indicate that satiation feeding was later phased out to healthy levels without undue difficulty, and the desired behaviors persisted.

Ayllon (1964) designed a token economy within which adult psychotics on a state hospital ward could progressively better their lives. Lists of behaviors for which tokens could be earned were posted and explained. Earned tokens could be exchanged for "good things" such as candy, cigarettes, clothing, cosmetics, passes, and a bed in a more desirable room. They could even serve as an indication that the patient was ready to leave the hospital. Facilities for rehabilitation of juvenile offenders have utilized this concept of "earning one's way" with remarkable success.

Personal, verbal, and social skills were set up as goal behaviors for a group of mentally retarded girls between the ages of eight and twenty-one living in "cottages" at Parsons State Hospital, Parsons, Kansas (Lent, 1968). Extensive programs of instruction and aid were developed to improve such skills as care of clothing, physical cleanliness, physical grooming, walking, sitting, appropriate verbal behavior, and social interaction. British halfpennies served as tokens for younger girls, while marks on a gridded point card were effective tokens for the older girls.

Immediate tangible reinforcement has also proved effective with groups in more academic settings. At the inception of a token system, an abrupt reduction occurred in the deviant behavior of a class of 17 nine-year-old emotionally disturbed children (O'Leary and Becker, 1967). Used as tokens were ratings, recorded in a small booklet, that could be traded for back-up reinforcers. Although the amount of tangible reinforcement was reduced, and the delay before exchange was permitted was lengthened, deviant behavior maintained at approximately one-eighth of its original or baseline rate.

A successful "engineered" classroom with diversified activity equipment for emotionally disturbed children is described by Hewett (1967). Each student picked up his individual work record card, ruled with 150 to 200 squares, as he entered in the morning, and received a maximum of 10 checkmarks for each 15 minute period. A teacher aide dispensed the marks for students functioning in the specified desired manner in the stimulating environment. Once a week, students exchanged completed work record cards for candy, small toys, and trinkets.

In one report (Birnbrauer, Bijou, Wolf, Kidder, and Tague, 1964), a class of mentally retarded children engaged in programmed learning activities in such areas as sight vocabulary, phonics, reading comprehension, cursive writing, addition, and time telling. Booklets with pages of varying values were ruled into squares. In looking them over, teachers made comments such as, "Your 2¢ page is almost full," or "You've completed your 5¢ page today—good for you." Filled pages were usually exchanged at the end of the day for a variety of edibles and trinkets of value equivalent to the page. Some children saved pages to apply toward a larger purchase or a trip to town. Most pupils earned about 2¢ per day in token value, and markedly increased the quality of their academic performances.

HOW TO BE A BEHAVIORALLY ORIENTED PRECISION TEACHER

It is evident from the above review that appropriate behavior change techniques have demonstrated substantial success in modifying selected behaviors of members of seriously disadvantaged clinical and academic populations, such as autistic and mentally retarded children. Some teachers, upon hearing about the powerful effects of token economies and other applications of reinforcement learning theory, rush right out to buy a bag of M & Ms and begin handing them out in class. This is, of course, by no means the way to begin.

If you are a teacher who wants to change behavior, you must first know what that behavior is. That is, you must "pinpoint" the behavior you want to accelerate or decelerate. Suppose that a pupil named George is a problem in your classroom. "To improve George's attitude toward work" is not a specific enough description of the change you desire to see, but "How many times George talks out in class when he hasn't been called on!" *is* a specific description of the behavior you would like to change, and it is pinpointed enough to allow the number of times that George "talks out" to be counted. And that is the next step in the behavior change process—to count and record the number of times that "talk out" occurs in your class. This will not be extra work for you, since any student can count George's "talk outs," but the best person to count George's "talk outs" is George. (Counting can be by using 49¢ push button supermarket counters, paper and pencil, or making marks on masking tape stuck to an arm.) After George has counted his total number of "talk outs," he can record them on a graph perhaps similar to the one below. (Special log paper is available on which the rate of any behavior may be plotted. Conversion to such rate graphs is not difficult and provides a more efficient record of behavior.)

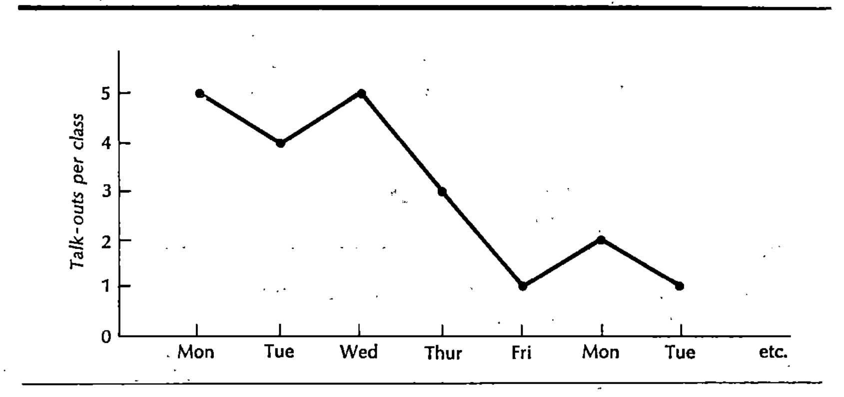

The mere fact that George is recording his own behavior may affect his number of "talk outs," as it did in this hypothetical example. However, suppose his "talk outs" remained at around five or six and you wanted to decelerate them. At this point, a third step in the process, called "change," should be invoked. Ideally, you and George should agree upon a plan for decelerating his "talk outs." Such a plan can involve almost anything, such as a sign on his desk to remind him, or a picture of a boy with his mouth open, or that he receives one M & M for each 10 minutes during which there is no "talk out," or that he has to stay in at play period one minute for each "talk out." The variety of plans for change is limited only by the creativity of the parties devising the plan.

Finally, if one plan does not work, try another, but continue to record the resultant behavior. These four steps to precision teaching and behavior control have been used extensively by Dr. Ogden Lindsley and his teachers in Kansas with great success. In review, the four steps to successful behavior change are: (1) Pinpoint; (2) Record; (3) Change; (4) Try, try again.

REFERENCES

Allen, K. E., Hart, B. M., Buell, J. S., Harris, F. R., and Wolf, M. M. Effects of social reinforcement on isolate behavior of a nursery school child. *Child Development,* 1964, *35,* 511–518.

Ayllon, T., and Michael, J. The psychiatric nurse as a behavioral engineer. *Journal of Experimental Analysis of Behavior,* 1959, *2,* 323–334.

Ayllon, T., and Haughton, E. Control of the behavior of schizophrenics by food. *Journal of Experimental Analysis of Behavior,* 1962, *5,* 343–352.

Ayllon, T. Intensive treatment of psychotic behavior by stimulus satiation and food reinforcement. *Behavior Research and Therapy,* 1963, *1,* 53–61.

Ayllon, T. Conditioning procedures in the rehabilitation of psychotic patients. Unpublished manuscript, 1964.

Ayllon, T. Some behavioral problems associated with eating in chronic schizophrenic patients. In L. P. Ullmann and L. Krasner, 1965.

Azrin, N. H., Pubin, H., O'Brien, F., Ayllon, T., and Roll, D. Behavioral engineering: Postural control by a portable operant apparatus. *Journal of Applied Behavior Analysis,* 1968, *1,* 99–108.

Azrin, N. H., and Lindsley, O. R. The reinforcement of cooperation between children. *Journal of Abnormal and Social Psychology,* 1956, *52,* 100–102.

Baer, D. M. Laboratory control of thumbsucking by withdrawal and representation of reinforcement. *Journal of Experimental Analysis of Behavior,* 1962, *5,* 525–528.

Bandura, A.. Ross, D., and Ross, S. A. Imitation of film-mediated aggressive models. *Journal of Abnormal and Social Psychology,* 1963, *66,* 3–11.

Barrett, B. Reduction in rate of multiple tics by free operant conditioning methods. *Journal of Nervous and Mental Disease,* 1962, *135,* 187–195.

Bijou, S. W., and Baer, D. M. (Eds.). *Child Development: Readings in experimental Analysis.* New York: Appleton-Century-Crofts, 1967.

Birnbrauer, J. S., Bijou, S. W., Wolf, M. M., Kidder, J. D., and Tague, C. A programmed instruction classroom for educable retardates. Unpublished manuscript, University of Washington, 1964.

Bond, I. K., and Hutchison, H. C. Application of reciprocal inhibition therapy to exhibitionism. *Canadian Medical Association Journal,* 1960, *83,* 23–25.

Brady, J. P., and Lind, D. L. Experimental analysis of hysterical blindness. *AMA Archives of General Psychiatry,* 1961, *4,* 331–339.

Crosson, J. E., and deJung, J. E. The experimental analysis of vocational behavior in severely retarded males. Final Report, Project No. 6–8066, Grant No. OEG 32–47–0230–6024, 1967.

Davison, G. The training of undergraduates as social reinforcers for autistic children. In L. P. Ullmann and L. Krasner, 1965.

Dulany, D. E. The place of hypotheses and intention: An analysis of verbal control in verbal conditioning. *Journal of Personality,* 1962, *30,* (2 Suppl. No. 6), 102–129.

Edwards, M., and Lilly, R. T. Operant conditioning: An application to behavioral problems in groups. *Mental Retardation,* 1966, *4,* 18–20.

Ferster, C. B., and DeMyer, M. K. A method of experimental analysis of the behavior of autistic children. *American Journal of Orthopsychiatry,* 1962, *32,* 89–98.

Ferster, C. B., Nurnberger, J. I., and Levitt, E. B. The control of eating. *Journal of Mathetics,* 1962, *1,* 87–109.

Flanagan, B., Goldiamond, I., and Azrin, N. Operant stuttering: The control of stuttering behavior through response-contingent consequences. *Journal of Experimental Analysis of Behavior,* 1958, *1,* 173–178.

Fuller, P. R. Operant conditioning of a vegetative human organism. *American Journal of Psychology,* 1949, *62,* 587–590.

Goldiamond, I. Stuttering and fluency as manipulatable operant response classes. In L. Krasner and L. P. Ullman, 1965.

Hall, V. R., Lund, D., and Jackson, D. Effects of teacher attention on study behavior. *Journal of Applied Behavior Analysis,* 1968, *1,* 1–12.

Harlow, H. F. The formation of learning sets. *The Psychological Review,* 1949, *56,* 51–65.

Hart, B. M., and Risley, T. R. Establishing use of descriptive adjectives in the spontaneous speech of disadvantaged preschool children. *Journal of Applied Behavior Analysis,* 1968, *1,* 109–120.

Hewett, F. M. Educational engineering with emotionally disturbed children. Unpublished manuscript. Santa Monica Unified School District, United States Office of Education, 1967.

Hingtgen, J. N., Sanders, Beverly J., and DeMyer, Marian K. Shaping cooperative responses in early childhood schizophrenics. In L. P. Ullmann and L. Krasner, 1965.

Hingtgen, J. N., and Trost, F. C., Jr. Shaping cooperative responses in early childhood schizophrenics: I. Reinforcement of mutual physical contact and vocal responses. In R. Ulrich, T. Stachnik, and J. Mabry, 1966.

Isaacs, W., Thomas, J., and Goldiamond, I. Application of operant conditioning to reinstate verbal behavior in psychotics. *Journal of Speech and Hearing Disorders,* 1960, 25, 8–12.

King, G. F., Armitage, S. G., and Filton, J. R. A therapeutic approach to schizophrenics of extreme pathology: An operant-interpersonal method. *Journal of Abnormal Social Psychology,* 1960, *61,* 276–286.

Krasner, L., and Ullmann, L. P. (Eds.). *Research in behavior modification.* New York: Holt, Rinehart and Winston, 1965.

Kushner, M. Desensitization of a post-traumatic phobia. In L. P. Ullmann and L. Krasner, 1965.

Lang, P. J. Behavior therapy with a case of nervous anorexia. In L. P. Ullmann and L. Krasner, 1965.

Lang, P. J., and Lazovik, A. D. Experimental desensitization of a phobia. *Journal of Abnormal and Social Psychology,* 1963, *66,* 519–525.

Lazarus, A. A. Group therapy of phobic disorders by systematic disensitization. *Journal of Abnormal and Social Psychology,* 1961, *63,* 504–510.

Lazarus, A. A. The treatment of a sexually inadequate man. In L. P. Ullmann and L. Krasner, 1965.

Lindsley, O. R. Precision teaching. Paper presented at Conference on Precision Teaching, University of Kansas, 1969.

Lent, J. R. Mimosa Cottage: Experiment in hope. Progress Reports, 1966–67, Parsons Research Center, Grant No. MR–1801A66, Public Health Service.

Lott. B. E., and Lott, A. J. The formation of positive attitude toward group members. *Journal of Abnormal and Social Psychology,* 1960, *61,* 297–300.

Lovass, O. I., Freitag, G., Gold, V. J., and Kassorla, I. C. Experimental studies in childhood schizophrenia: I. Analysis of self-destructive behavior. In S. W. Bijou and D. M. Baer, 1967.

Madsen, C. H., Jr. Positive reinforcement in the toilet training of a normal child: A case report. In L. P. Ullmann and L. Krasner, 1965.

Meyerson, L., Kerr, N., and Michael, J. L. Behavior modification in rehabilitation. In S. W. Bijou and D. M. Baer, 1967.

O'Leary, K. D., and Becker, W. C. Behavior modification of an adjustment class: A token reinforcement program. *Exceptional Children,* 1967, *33,* 637–642.

Patterson, G. R. A learning theory approach to the treatment of a school phobic child. In L. P. Ullmann and L. Krasner, 1965.

Premack, D. Toward empirical behavior laws: I. Positive reinforcement. *The Psychological Review,* 1959, *66,* 219–233.

Rheingold, H., Gewirtz, J. L., and Ross, H. Social conditioning of vocalizations in the infant. *Journal of Comparative and Physiological Psychology,* 1959, *52,* 68–73.

Richard, H. C., and Dinoff, M. A follow-up note on "verbal manipulation in a psychotherapeutic relationship." *Psychological Reports,* 1962, *11,* 506.

Rickard, H. C., and Mundy, M. Direct manipulation of stuttering behavior: An experimental-clinical approach. In L. P. Ullmann and L. Krasner, 1965.

Risley, T., and Wolf, M. M. Experimental manipulation of autistic behaviors and generalization into the home. In R. Ulrich, T. Stachnik, and J. Mabry, 1966.

Saslow, G. A case history of attempted behavior manipulation in a psychiatric ward. In L. Krasner and L. P. Ullmann, 1965.

Skinner, B. F. *Science and human behavior.* New York: Free Press, 1953.

Staats, A. W. (Ed.). *Human learning.* New York: Holt, Rinehart and Winston, 1964.

Ullmann, L. P., and Krasner L. (Eds.). *Case studies in behavior modification.* New York: Holt, Rinehart and Winston, 1965.

Ulrich, R., Stachnik, T., and Mabry, J. (Eds.). *Control of human behavior.* Glenview, Ill.: Scott, Foresman, 1966.

Verplanck, W. S. Unaware of where's awareness: Some verbal operants-notates, moments, and notants. In C. W. Eriksen (Ed.), *Behavior and Awareness.* Durham: Duke University Press, 1962.

Wahler, R. G., Winkle, G. H., Peterson, R. F., and Morrison, D. C. Mothers as behavior therapists for their own children. *Behavior Research and Therapy,* 1965, *3,* 113–134.

Williams, C. D. The elimination of tantrum behavior by extinction procedures. *Journal of Abnormal and Social Psychology,* 1959, *59, 269.*

Wolf, M. M., Risley, T., and Mees, H. Application of operant conditioning procedures to the behavior problems of an autistic child. *Behavior Research and Therapy,* 1964, *1,* 305–312.

Wolf, M. M., Birnbrauer, J. S., Williams, T., and Lawler, J. A note on apparent extinction of the vomiting behavior of a retarded child. In L. P. Ullmann and L. Krasner, 1965.

Zeilberger, J., Sampen, S. E., and Sloane, H. N. Modification of a child's problem behaviors in the home with the mother as therapist. *Journal of Applied Behavior Analysis,* 1968, *1,* 47–53.

EVALUATIVE DATA

INTRODUCTION

The Behavior Change Process was designed to utilize principles of operant learning and/or behavior shaping. Richard Walls' review of the research literature presents compelling evidence that certain principles of operant learning are effective in changing behavior. The text consists of linear programmed instruction combining constructed linear and multiple-response frames. The reading level is eighth grade.

Programmed instruction is based on the assumption that learning efficiency is increased by presenting subject matter to the student in a series of logically ordered, small steps, requiring the student to be actively involved in the learning process by making a correct response to each step, and reinforcing his responses by providing him with immediate feedback.

Arguments supporting programmed instruction are that the student learns more efficiently by being actively involved in the learning process, and that the immediate feedback or reinforcement principle combines with involvement to make learning a more meaningful experience (Mink, Smith, Harmon, 1963). Ripple (1963) demonstrated that active involvement of the pupil is the more compelling force in programming. Ripple selected 240 subjects and assigned them to four groups by using a 50-item achievement test relating to the eventual criterion measures. His method, sample size, and statistical tests are indicative of reliable research. Holland (1960) compared three conditions, and his findings, too, support the active involvement contention. In his study, one group used standard programmed instruction, with feedback; a second group also used the standard program but received no feedback following their responses; and a third group simply read complete statements. The third group made about twice as many errors on a criterion test as did the first two groups. In a program with a low error rate the reinforcement provided through immediate feedback may be without significant effect in promoting learning. Unfortunately, Holland provides us little information on the size of the treatment groups, and no statistical analysis is reported.

Woodruff, Falkz, and Wagner (1966) found that differences in learner characteristics may have an effect on learning performance. With fourth, fifth, and ninth grade subjects, learning ability, ability to read, and selected personality traits are functionally related to performance. Allowing learners to progress at their own rate does not meet all the problems of personality differences in learning performance.

Flynn (1966) studied the influence of programmed learning on achievers and underachievers in educational psychology classes. Subjects were selected using past class grades and class participation for criteria. He found that achievers using programmed instruction gained significantly over those using conventional classroom methods. Underachievers did equally well regardless of method. Armenia (1967) found that programmed learning has been highly motivating for culturally deprived high school students, who are frequently turned off by a middle-class educational system. Although these students were underachievers, they were not incapable of doing well.

Programmed learning, then, cannot be said to solve all learning problems, but it has been shown to be effective for the majority of personality types, including achievers and students considered to be culturally disadvantaged, though not necessarily slow learners. Limited reading ability, and limited ability to compare or differentiate answers adversely affects the success of slow learners in programmed instruction.

The Behavior Change Process was designed specifically to assist vocational rehabilitation instructors in an understanding of reinforcement principles, and to teach the instructors a procedure for determining action appropriate for strengthening or modifying behavior. However, the manual is also an effective device for helping public school teachers and counselors achieve similar goals. With this in mind, the manual was field tested both on samples of vocational rehabilitation instructors and on educational psychology students in the process of becoming teachers and counselors. It has also been read by several public school teachers. Although controlled research has not been conducted with this latter population, self-report evaluations are very favorable.

Field testing *The Behavior Change Process* on samples of vocational rehabilitation instructors, supervisors, graduate students in counseling and undergraduate educational psychology students filled the dual objectives of providing an understanding of reinforcement principles in operation and establishing a procedure for modifying client behavior. The success of the objectives was examined by pre-, post-, and retention test data as well as subjective evaluations.

INSTRUMENTS

The programmed manual entitled *The Behavior Change Process* was designed for use by vocational instructors, teachers, and counselors as an aid to improve behavior in the classroom. The basic principles of behavior change, (principles of behavior theory, and programmed instruction that includes case examples) are covered. Research notes substantiating the principles explained in the manual follow the text. Each of the 169 frames of programmed instruction has been read by over 40 subjects, who recorded the frames they had answered incorrectly. Frames missed by more than 4 subjects were checked to insure that the frames were correctly and clearly written. Forty subjects evaluated the program on a questionnaire.

TESTS

Test A contains in random order the seven steps of *The Behavior Change Process* that are to be placed by the subject in the proper sequence. It was developed as a pre- and post-test measure to test understanding of the sequential process of changing behavior.

Test B was a 23 item multiple-choice test administered as a pre-, post-, and retention measure. When Test B was originally given as a pre-test to subjects, it contained 30 multiple-choice items. Of that pool, an item analysis was conducted to obtain a difficulty index for each item. All items missed by less than 25% and more than 75% of the subjects were eliminated. Twenty-three items remained for the final post-test and retention test. The function of the test was not only to assess mastery over operant learning principles, but to test the effectiveness of learning how to apply these principles to examples. Therefore, the test was separated into 11 concept items referring to an understanding of reinforcement, operant learning, shaping, extinction, and punishment, and 12 process items referring to various situations in which alternative solutions were given for a concrete problem.

PROCEDURE

1. VOCATIONAL INSTRUCTORS

Subjects in Group A were 24 male and female vocational instructors and supervisors at a vocational rehabilitation center, designated center number 1. Group B subjects were six male supervisors and counselors at another vocational rehabilitation center, designated center number 2; Group C consisted of 30 male and female instructors also at center number 2.

METHOD

Subjects in Groups A, B, and C were instructed that the *The Behavior Change Process* was a manual that might help staff members better understand and more effectively deal with client behavior in the rehabilitation center. It was also explained that reading the manual was to be completed in one day in a controlled setting for research purposes. Subjects took pre-tests A and B and then worked through the manual at their own speed, which varied from four to eight hours. Subjects answered each frame of the constructed-response programmed text and recorded the frames they answered incorrectly.

When each subject finished the manual, he took post-tests A and B, but was not shown the correct answers. A follow-up study was completed two weeks later, at the time when subjects took the retention test and evaluated the effectiveness of the manual.

2. GRADUATE CLASS IN COUNSELING

The subjects were ten students enrolled in a graduate class in Counseling and Guidance at West Virginia University. Most of the subjects had previously been introduced to the principles of operant learning and behavior shaping.

Subjects were given Pre-test B in class and asked to read *The Behavior Change Process* in the week before the next class session. At the next class meeting, subjects were given Post-test B and asked to evaluate the test items subjectively and also to evaluate the program.

3. EDUCATIONAL PSYCHOLOGY CLASS

The subjects were 40 students enrolled in an introductory educational psychology class at West Virginia University. This course was entirely individualized and students were able to work at their own rates, and the class was divided into several sections by pre- and post-criterion tests. During the time that *The Behavior Change Process* was being introduced to the class, each subject studying the educational psychology learning unit involving the principles of operant learning and reinforcement. Experimental groups were made up of volunteers from the class or subjects who had not passed a criterion test in the Educational Psychology learning unit and for whom the manual was mandatory reading. These experimental subjects worked through *The Behavior Change Process* manual.

METHOD

Subjects in experimental groups were given pre-tests A and B and then told to read *The Behavior Change Process* manual at home checking each frame for incorrect responses and recording them on a separate sheet. At the time the subjects turned back in the answer sheet and manual, post-tests A and B were administered individually to them.

In the instructional period, the subjects were told that they would be participating in an experiment, and that the manual would be helpful for learning operant conditioning and reinforcement as well.

RESULTS

The 23-item multiple choice test (Test B) scores showed a significant increase in learning from pre- to post-testing. Pre-, post- and retention test mean scores on Test B were evaluated using a T-test for correlated data. There were no significant differences between post-test scores and retention scores. See the results in Tables 1 and 2 below.

TABLE 1

PRE-, POST-, AND RETENTION MEAN SCORES OF 23-ITEM MULTIPLE-CHOICE TEST (TEST B)

	Center 2 Instructors $N=18$	*Center 2 Supervisors* $N=6$	*Center 1 Instructors* $N=19$	*Ed. Psy. Class* $N=35$	*C & G 303* $N=10$
Pre-	$\bar{X}=10.9$	$\bar{X}=16.3$	$\bar{X}=11.7$	$\bar{X}=12.4$	$\bar{X}=15.2$
Post-	$\bar{X}=16.8$	$\bar{X}=20.8$	$\bar{X}=16.2$	$\bar{X}=17.7$	$\bar{X}=18.7$
Diff.	+5.9	+4.5	+4.5	+5.3	+3.5
Reten.	$\bar{X}=16.6$	$\bar{X}=19.9$	$\bar{X}=16.9$	———	———

TABLE 2

T-SCORES, CORRELATION, AND SIGNIFICANCE LEVELS OF PRE- TO POST- TESTS ON MULTIPLE CHOICE (TEST B)

	Degrees of Freedom	*Correlation*	*T-score*	*Level*
Center 2 supervisors	5	$r=.57$	$t=6.0$	.01
Center 2 instructors	17	$r=.65$	$t=6.28$	.001
Center 1 instructors	18	$r=.84$	$t=7.50$	.001
C & G 303	9	$r=.77$	$t=7.40$	.001
Ed. Psy. class	34, 22	———	$t=23.04$	.001

Scores on the 7-item sequence test (Test A) also showed a significant gain in knowledge from pre- to post-testing. Mean scores are shown in Table 3.

TABLE 3

MEAN SCORES ON PRE- AND POST-TESTS OF TEST A (7-ITEM SEQUENCE TEST)

	Center 2 Instructors $N=26$	*Center 2 Supervisors* $N=6$	*Center 1 Instructors* $N=15$	*Ed. Psy. Class* $N=40$
Pre-	$\bar{X}=3.3$	$\bar{X}=5.6$	$\bar{X}=4.7$	$\bar{X}=4.8$
Post-	$\bar{X}=6.0$	$\bar{X}=7.0$	$\bar{X}=6.1$	$\bar{X}=6.3$
Diff.	+2.7	+1.4	+1.4	+1.3

Most of the 40 subjects who evaluated the program from a questionnaire believed the program helped them recognize aspects of their own classroom behavior and attitudes they had not recently considered. Included in the new insights were several comments to the effect that subjects now recognize many forms of negative reinforcers they had used which they can no longer justify. They also emphasized an increased understanding of the power of positive reinforcement. Many subjects found they are now more observant of students' behavior and attitudes. The majority of subjects commented that the material was readily applicable to their own classroom situation.

Scores from 45 pre-tests and 52 post-tests of the 23-item multiple-choice tests (Test B) were evaluated by separating out the 11 concept items and 12 process items. It was shown that the process items, or items involving practical application of *The Behavior Change Process,* demonstrated retention superior to the conceptual items.

TABLE 4

NUMBER OF TIMES 12 PROCESS ITEMS AND 11 CONCEPT ITEMS WERE MISSED ON A 23-ITEM MULTIPLE CHOICE TEST (TEST B)

	Pre-Test *Process*	$N=45$ *Concept*	*Post-Test* *Process*	$N=52$ *Concept*
Mean	$\bar{X}=22.08$	$\bar{X}=25.27$	$\bar{X}=9.09$	$\bar{X}=16.91$
Median	$M=21$	$M=27$	$M=8$	$M=15$
Modes	$Mo=17$	$Mo=26,27,33$	$Mo=5,8,17$	$Mo=11,15$

Due to the individualized nature of the educational psychology class, the test data on that sample were not completely controlled. The multiple-choice scores on pre- and post-test data of both Tests A and B suggest trends entirely consistent with trends found among vocational supervisors and instructors—that is, students who had been exposed to conventional materials on the same topic still demonstrated significant improvement. Mean differences still improved over four points from pre- to post-test scores. These data were consistent for both tests, A and B.

Pre-test scores were as high for supervisors who had a background in operant learning as were the post-test scores for the other groups who took Test B. The graduate counseling class, who also had been introduced to the material, had high mean scores compared to the other groups. However, it was then seen that the gain for supervisors and the graduate class from pre- to post-testing was still highly significant (< .001), indicating that a large degree of learning still occurred. We think the increase is particularly important because it reflects a change in the precision of thinking about the application of behavior change principles in terms of process, conceptual understanding, and direct application.

Various strategies were used by the institutions in applying *The Behavior Change Process*. With our students in the educational psychology classes and at the rehabilitation center 1, individual teachers attempted to apply the principles on an individual student basis and managed to do so with some success. However, in some instances, a program which was beginning to be successful was interrupted.

For example, one of the instructors at the center 1 noticed a student attempting to get attention for wearing to class shorter skirts than were allowed. The instructor had ignored saying anything to the girl when she wore short skirts and praised her when her skirts were an appropriate length. Within a week she began to wear longer skirts. But one day a supervisor (who had not read the program) noticed her wearing a short skirt, pulled her out of class, and suspended her activities for three days. He also reprimanded the instructor. The achievements made by the instructor were completely undermined by the supervisor's punitive action.

By contrast to individual application at the center 1, center 2 required every staff member from dishwasher to director to read, discuss, and apply behavior change process principles to their clients. With all significant people modifying clients' behavior in the same way, results were quicker and more lasting.

This author had spent one day weekly for 20 weeks in an elementary and a junior school applying behavior change principles to a six-grade class and a ninth-grade class referred for their particularly disruptive behavior. Over the weeks the teachers involved with the sixth-graders read *The Behavior Change Process,* discussed it, and applied its concepts in their classroom with excellent results. The sixth-graders have become noticeably more responsible, more positive in their attitudes toward themselves, and they demonstrate more concern for their friends. As a result of this more harmonious atmosphere, their learning has also increased, as demonstrated by test scores and grades. For the first time in years, parents of this group became involved with the school in a positive manner. They became interested in the improved behavior of their children, and formed adult evening-study groups and parents groups to better organize the community.

At the junior high school, however, the teachers worked in a more rigid atmosphere, and saw new ideas as a threat to their teaching competency. The ninth-grade teachers refused to participate in discussions, or to agree to try new plans of positive reinforcements in classes with poor behavior. Although the ninth-grade students are beginning to be responsible in spite of the negative attitudes of their teachers, there has been little significant change in their actions. In the ninth-grade group, new plans of action have been decided upon frequently, usually contingent on teacher support and reinforcement; the teachers of the classes where the students had been particularly disruptive refused, however, to reward positive behavior, and so there has been little change and very little learning within the ninth-grade class this year.

The above cases demonstrate the need for a cooperative program among all the significant people involved with students —the teachers, administrators, parents, and other students. Although change can occur without total cooperation, it takes much longer and is much more difficult. The effectiveness of the *Behavior Change Process* as a pedagogical device for teaching the behavior modification process has been clearly established. The evidence in support of the viability of the reinforcement learning process is substantial and compelling. The data suggest a reliable process well taught.

REFERENCES

Armenia, J. Effectiveness of programmed learning as homework for culturally deprived high school students. *Psychological Reports,* 1967, *20,* Book 3, Part 1, 785–786.

Flynn, J. T. The influence of programmed instruction upon learning in educational psychology. *Journal of Educational Research,* 1966, *59,* Book 9, 387–391.

Holland, J. Design and use of a teaching machine program. Paper read at American Psychological Association Annual Convention, September, 1960.

Mink, O. G., Smith, Wm. R., and Harmon, Donald E. The training of technical representatives through programmed instruction. Mimeographed Report, Xerox Corporation, Rochester, New York, July, 1964, 8 pages.

Ripple, R. E. Comparison of the effectiveness of a programmed text with three other methods of presentation. *Psychological Reports,* 1963, *12,* 227–237.

Woodruff, A. B., Faltz, C., and Wagner, D. Effects of learner characteristics on programmed learning performance. *Psychology in the Schools,* 1966, *3,* Part 1, 72–77.

POST-TESTS

The following questions will test your knowledge of the steps in the behavior change process. There are three tests. Post-test A is identical to Pre-test A. Post-test C is the same as Pre-test B. We hope you will see an improvement when you compare your scores on Post-test A and C with your scores on the Pre-tests.

In Post-test B you will find one question on each page. Answer each question in sequence. After you have completed each question to your satisfaction, turn the page and go on the next question. Please do not turn back to a question once you have answered it.

Post-test C is also used for the retention test. All items have been field-tested, and it is the author's opinion that Post-test C is the most accurate and complete test of the knowledge learned directly from the course material. Instructors may wish to use only Post-test C or all Post-tests, or to compare Post-test A and C with the Pre-tests and retention test. The retention test is best utilized when given approximately two weeks after the Post-tests.

POST-TEST A

Place the following in the most logical sequence to change behavior.

_______ Identify the behavior that you wish to eliminate and identify the new behavior that you wish to strengthen; hold a conference with the student.

_______ Identify the possible reinforcers for the undesirable behavior and determine who or what is providing the reinforcement for the undesirable behavior.

_______ Maintain the new behavior by using positive reinforcement moving from a continuous reinforcement schedule to an occasional reinforcement schedule.

_______ Obtain suggestions from the student about ways to change his behavior; explain your own objections to his behavior; offer your own suggestions; consult with guidance services.

_______ Reshape the new behavior (if the old behavior recurs) and/or re-examine your past actions in the behavior change process.

_______ Decide upon a reinforcer that you think will strengthen the new behavior, and withhold the reinforcer for the undesirable behavior (extinction) or suppress the old behavior.

_______ Shape the new behavior.

POST-TEST B

1. What actions do you take in the first step of the behavior change process?

   Identify:

   Identify:

   Discuss:

2. What actions do you take in the second step of the behavior change process when you are holding a conference with the student?

Offer suggestions from:

Consult with:

Offer suggestions from:

3. If the student can't offer suggestions of his own as to how to change his behavior, what should the instructor do?

4. During the teacher-student conference, how can the instructor get the student himself to participate in the process of bringing about a change in his behavior?

5. If the student had no suggestions to offer, the group wasn't very helpful, and you yourself had difficulty interpreting the old behavior and making suggestions, what other sources could you consult for further suggestions?

6. You have identified the undesirable behavior and the desirable behavior you would like to strengthen instead, and you have discussed the student's behavior with him (step 1); you have also obtained suggestions from the student as to ways he feels he can change his own behavior, and you have obtained any needed information from outside resource people and have made suggestions of your own (step 2); what do you identify in step 3 before you can take any further action?

7. a. What action do you take to weaken or extinguish the old undesirable behavior?

   b. What action do you take before you can strengthen new behavior?

8. After you decide upon the reinforcer for the desirable behavior (step 4), how do you bring about the new behavior?

9. What reinforcement schedule should be used (that is, how often should you provide reinforcement) to shape new behavior?

10. **a.** After the desirable behavior is shaped, what is the next step for making certain that the desirable behavior continues to occur?

b. After a new behavior has already been shaped, what reinforcement schedule should be used to make certain the behavior continues to occur?

11. Once behavior has been shaped, what action(s) would you take if the old, undesirable behavior recurred?

and/or

POST-TEST C

INSTRUCTIONS: Circle the most correct alternative.

1. The first step in changing behavior of a student is to

   a. teach a new behavior.
   b. identify which behaviors you wish to eliminate and strengthen.
   c. extinguish or suppress undesirable behavior.
   d. discuss the problem behavior with the student.

2. Punishment may be successful in suppressing undesirable behavior, but it has possible side effects. Which of these alternatives is *not* considered a side effect of punishment?

   a. Punishment may be emotionally damaging to self-esteem.
   b. Punishment must be extremely drastic to significantly affect behavior.
   c. Punishment may be reinforcing the undesirable behavior.
   d. Punishment teaches the limits of acceptable behavior.

3. When holding a conference with a student about his undesirable behavior, what action can be taken then to encourage change?

   a. Punish him for his undesirable behavior.
   b. Obtain suggestions from him about ways to change his behavior.
   c. Praise him for the positive behavior he shows.
   d. Explain your own objections to his behavior.

4. Extinction of a student's behavior may best occur when

   a. the behavior is punished sharply and immediately.
   b. mild aversive stimuli is used so it is not damaging to the student.
   c. events that reinforce the undesirable behavior are removed.
   d. more positive behavior is reinforced.

5. When a student occasionally disrupts the classroom by making wiscracks, which alternative is the best to handle him?
   a. Report him to the counselor.
   b. Send him out of class.
   c. Ignore his behavior.
   d. Tell him to keep quiet.
6. Behavior is often changed through "shaping." Which of the following statements about shaping behavior is **not** true?
   a. Shaping is a gradual, training process.
   b. Behavior is made up of unconnected units.
   c. Desired behavior can be developed in a series of steps.
   d. Correct behavior is built up in small steps and strengthened until desirable behavior is reached.
7. If desirable new behavior in established and slips back into undesirable behavior, what action should first be taken?
   a. Ignore undesirable behavior.
   b. Reshape desirable new behavior.
   c. Punish undesirable behavior.
   d. Look for another desirable behavior.
8. Which is the most effective method of increasing the likelihood that a student will respond in a given way?
   a. Extinguish other responses.
   b. Have other students respond that way.
   c. Make the stimulus clear for the response.
   d. Reinforce similar responses.
9. The cause of recurrence of a particular misbehavior in school lies in
   a. effects of previous misbehavior.
   b. sibling rivalry.
   c. personality traits.
   d. the student's home background.
10. Continuous reinforcement schedules would be used in the behavior change process when
    a. new behavior is being shaped.
    b. new behavior is being maintained.
    c. undesirable behavior is being extinguished.
    d. behavior is being suppressed.

11. In reshaping (for the second time) new behavior, what action should *not* be taken?

   a. Reinforce desirable new behavior.
   b. Discuss the problem with the student.
   c. Punish undesirable behavior.
   d. Reconsider the reinforcements that were used.

12. Learning is a process that always brings about

   a. behavior that aids the person in his adjustment.
   b. improvements in the person's ways of perceiving or responding.
   c. increased variability in the person.
   d. changes in the way the person responds.

13. Occasional reinforcement schedules in changing behavior would be used when

   a. extinguishing an undesirable behavior.
   b. maintaining a new behavior.
   c. shaping a new behavior.
   d. suppressing behavior.

14. For reinforcement to be the most effective in learning, reinforcing experience should occur

   a. after a lapse of a few days in order to permit the learned material to become established.
   b. immediately after the response.
   c. simultaneously with the learning.
   d. immediately before application is made.

15. Which of the statements about punishment is *not* true?

   a. Undesirable behavior is best weakened when the reinforcers which strengthen it are withheld.
   b. Punishment is the most effective way to weaken undesirable behavior.
   c. Punishment may temporarily stop undesirable behavior but may not change the behavior pattern.
   d. Behavior may be changed using methods other than punishment.

16. When a student is learning a new desirable behavior at school, he will learn it most quickly if he is reinforced

a. occasionally (randomly).
b. frequently.
c. at regular intervals.
d. continuously.

17. Learning takes place as a result of the individual's attempt to

a. improve himself.
b. conform to the expectations of his society.
c. satisfy multiple motives and purposes.
d. project his self-esteem.

18. After a student has learned a desirable behavior, he should be reinforced

a. occasionally.
b. once out of every two times the behavior occurs.
c. whenever the behavior occurs.
d. not at all.

19. Which of the following steps of the behavioral change process is out of place?

a. Identify behavior to be changed and new behavior.
b. Hold conference with student.
c. Identify possible reinforcers.
d. Withhold reinforcer for undesirable behavior.
e. none

21. You have determined some final behavior you want to strengthen during the early stages of the process of shaping you must reinforce

a. any response at all.
b. a response that approaches the desirable behavior.
c. only the final desirable behavior.
d. positive and negative behavior both.

22. Repeated failure to reinforce a previously learned response is most likely to lead to

a. the development of a strong habit.
b. the elimination of an habitual response.
c. striving for unrealistic goals.
d. experimental neurosis.
e. anxiety.

23. After desirable behavior has been learned, the undesirable behavior may occasionally reoccur. By not calling attention to the undesirable behavior, what method of controlling behavior is being used?

a. No behavior is being controlled at all.
b. punishment (negative reinforcement)
c. reinforcement of undesirable behavior
d. extinction

24. In the final stages of the shaping process (after new behavior exists), reinforcement should be given

a. occasionally.
b. whenever a response approaches desired behavior.
c. only when the new behavior occurs.
d. at regular intervals.

ANSWER KEY

POST-TEST A

1, 3, 6, 2, 7, 4, 5

ANSWER KEY

POST-TEST B

1. **Identify** the undesirable behavior.
Identify the desirable behavior that should occur instead.
Discuss the student's behavior with him.

2. Obtain suggestions from the student himself, and/or class.
   Consult with outside resource people (guidance, psychological).
   Offer suggestions yourself to the student.
3. The instructor should offer his own suggestions.
4. The instructor should ask the student to offer suggestions.
5. guidance and psychological services
6. **Identify** what is reinforcing the undesirable behavior.
7. a. **Withhold** the reinforcer for the undesirable behavior (extinguish old behavior)
   b. **Decide** upon the reinforcer for the desirable behavior (reinforce new behavior)
8. Shape the desirable behavior (apply continuous reinforcement at first to behavior which comes closer and closer to some final behavior).
9. a **continuous** reinforcement schedule
10. a. **Maintain** the behavior.
    b. an **occasional** reinforcement schedule (reinforce the behavior now and then)
11. **Reshape** her behavior,
    and/or
    Reexamine your past actions in the behavior change process

ANSWER KEY

POST-TEST C

1. b	**7.** b	**13.** b	**19.** e
2. d	**8.** d	**14.** b	**20.** b
3. b	**9.** a	**15.** b	**21.** b
4. c	**10.** a	**16.** d	**22.** d
5. c	**11.** c	**17.** c	**23.** a
6. b	**12.** d	**18.** a	

INDEX

Set in Linotype Optima
Format by Jared Eddy
Composition by V & M Typographical, Inc.
Printed by The Murray Printing Company
Manufactured by The Murray Printing Company

70 71 72 73 7 6 5 4 3 2